FLAVOUR FIRST

Delicious food to bring the family back to the table

MARY SUE WAISMAN

Flavour First – Delicious food to bring the family back to the table
by Mary Sue Waisman

First Printing – July 2007

All About Food Nutrition Consulting
Fall River, Nova Scotia B2T 1S6
902-576-5025
mswaisman@yahoo.com

National Library of Canada Cataloguing in Publication Data

Waisman, Mary Sue (Mary Suzanne), 1957-
Flavour first : delicious food to bring the family back to the table / Mary Sue Waisman.

Includes index.
ISBN 978-0-9783452-0-4

1. Cookery. I. Title.

TX714.W25 2007 641.5 C2007-903415-2

Photography by Ted Coldwell, Coldwell Photography, Halifax, Nova Scotia
Production and editing by 4th Floor Press, Inc., Calgary, Alberta www.4thfloorpress.com
Cover Design by Brian Danchuk, Brian Danchuk Design, Regina

Printed in Canada by:
Centax Books, a division of PrintWest Communications Ltd.
Publishing Co-ordinator: Iona Glabus
1150 Eighth Avenue, Regina, Saskatchewan, Canada S4R 1C9
(306) 525-2304 FAX: (306) 757-2439
centax@printwest.com www.centaxbooks.com

ACKNOWLEDGMENTS

I'll bet most cookbook authors who 'go it alone' are comforted by knowing that a whole bunch of people are behind you humming words of encouragement and support. No cookbook effort is ever really done alone. I express my heartfelt gratitude to my grandparents, parents, aunts, uncles, and cousins who joined me at dinner tables over the years and inspired me to realize that great things really do happen at the dinner table.

This book is as much written by my mother, Philomena, as it is by me. Her love of cooking and caring for people with food is endless. I'm grateful to my father, Chester, for his unending love and support in pretty much everything I've ever done in life and for bringing home those special donuts every Thursday night. I thank my husband, David, who never once questioned my ability or intentions in writing this book, and to my children, Meredith and Phillip, for enduring countless meals and answering the never-ending question: 'how does it taste'? I'm grateful to my long time friend, Denise Graven, who challenged every word I ever wrote, and to Chef Janet Lewis for testing new creations.

TABLE OF CONTENTS

INTRODUCTION

FLAVOUR FIRST is the motto I live by when I cook. While food is necessary to nourish both the body and the soul, it does a much better job of both when it's full of flavour. When food tastes delicious, it's easy to eat well; when food tastes delicious, it's easy to linger at the table, savour the taste, and indulge in conversation.

Bringing families back to the dinner table is something worth talking about. Families are dining together less often for many reasons. Watch any family in action these days and you'll see they're torn in several different directions. Our busy lives are ruining our ability to sit down to the table and eat together – and not without consequence. My opinions about the importance of dining together are born out by recent research showing that there are good reasons to eat together. Families who dine together more often have less family tension and stress and better communication. Teens from families who often dine together say that their parents are more proud of them. These teens also smoke less and have lower rates of alcohol and illegal substance abuse.

Families also dine together less often because we are losing our ability to cook! Cooking skills are not being handed down the way they were 'in the old days'. If we're not careful, I believe we will soon be in a cooking crisis. Not that it's necessary that we all know how to make a crème brûlée, but if we put a generation forward that can't scramble eggs, make a pot of soup from turkey bones, roast some beef, or bake a cake, I fear what will become of the cooking skills and eating habits of generations to come.

We're faced with thousands of new food items on the grocery store shelves every year. I'm just as grateful as the next person for pre-washed spinach, packaged red Thai curry paste, frozen mango, and the occasional ready-roasted chicken. New food items can save time, make it easy to try new tastes, and provide great nutrition. But we would be doing ourselves a great disservice if we came to rely solely on pre-packed, precooked foods for our everyday lives. While some of the flavour may be there, there's a great loss in not learning how to plan a meal, seek out the ingredients, enhance the flavour, and then enjoy the meal at the table.

Cooking shows are one of the hottest genres on television right now – but don't just be an observer; learn from the best and then pick up a few ingredients, a pot, a wooden spoon, and get cooking! There has been a tremendous surge in home renovations, gardening, etc. We should add cooking to the growing list of do-it-yourself trends. Don't just watch the cooking shows, get creative in your own kitchen; take pride in the accomplishment of doing it yourself. Experience the satisfaction of bringing your family and friends to your table to enjoy your food and one another's company. This wonderful feeling will make you want to cook again and again!

Great things can happen at a dinner table, and great tasting, flavourful food is the way to get people there. While growing up, it was easy to say "Right away" when Mom said "Please come to the table". Those words from my mother have echoed through my life for nearly fifty years, and I find myself repeating them daily with my family and friends. While growing up, I have fond memories of my family dinner table. Dad was often already at work by the time my brother and I arrived at the breakfast table, but Mom was usually there in the morning to put something simple yet delicious in our stomachs before heading off to school with a brown bag lunch. On the odd time that I came home for lunch, I always found the same sight: Dad sitting at the table, reading the paper or doing a crossword puzzle, and eating homemade soup right out of the pot. After all, "Why dirty another dish when the pot worked fine and kept the soup warm?"

Supper time was special as we finally got to see our dad, who had worked hard all day selling appliances and furniture. Thursdays were really special as Dad would always bring home donuts from our favourite bakery. My special treat was called a 'half-moon' – a cake-like cookie that was frosted half with chocolate and half with white frosting to resemble both sides of the moon (see recipe on page 166). The weekends brought wonderful bounty to the table, surrounded with aunts, uncles, and cousins, and the good fortune of grandparents from both sides of the family – a truly tight family unit where no one wandered off till much later in life.

These may not sound like great things, but I've realized something over the years: sitting at the table was not just a time to nourish our bodies, it was a precious time to nourish our souls and instil family values. We shared events of the day, sought counsel (without even realizing it) on the tribulations of our life, laughed with each other, celebrated birthdays and anniversaries, and felt rather lost when one of us wasn't present. Without knowing it, the table became the place where we all learned about life.

History also teaches us that great things can happen at the 'table.' If you happen to be a believer in The Last Supper, you'll know that great things happened at that table. Imagine how history could have been different if the guests at the table had to run off to an Olympic event! Closer to home, Canadian history shows us that during the settling of Charlottetown, Prince Edward Island, the hospitality at the table was instrumental in building the nation: "Canadian hospitality was so lavish that the delegates were on board eating and drinking until late in the evening... sufficient unity persuaded the gathering to permit the unofficial proclamation of the new nation." E.W.P. Bolger, "Nation Building at Charlottetown" Canada's Smallest Province. Charlottetown, The Prince Edward Island Centennial Commission, 1973, 135-155.

I can't claim to build nations or religions at my dinner table, but nonetheless, great things also happen there. Rare is the day when we don't have a friend of one of my children joining us at the table. Not long ago, my daughter and several of her teenage friends showed up for dinner with two large zucchinis in tow. They wanted me to make a traditional fried zucchini dish that they had tried at our home months ago. I felt honoured and seized the opportunity to pass on a flavourful, traditional item. I pulled out the ingredients and proceeded to teach them all how to make it. My children know their friends are always welcome to share a meal with us and share a little bit about their lives. The same is true for 'grown up' friends – it's always easy to set another place for someone who drops by, even if it's left-over night!

Flavour First will give you wonderful food ideas to help bring your family back to the table. I hope you enjoy making and sharing these foods with your family and friends, and please be sure to enjoy them at the table.

Cooking and Nutrition Fundamentals

The 'fun' in 'fun'damentals – the top 5 fun tips to know about cooking and eating:

- **Tantalize your taste buds.** Try new foods from around the world and let your kids, friends, and family try them too. It may be easiest to try the flavours at an ethnic restaurant to see what you like. Then, take your adventuresome spirit into the kitchen and try to make some of them. So what if it doesn't work the first time? There's always another day to try another recipe!

- **Choose from thousands of fun gadgets and utensils.** Buy only what you really need and test it first. Do you really need that shrimp de-veiner? cherry pitter? pineapple cutter? Stock your kitchen carefully, otherwise you'll be cluttering your kitchen and soon be sending the items to the garage sale table!

- **Keep cookbooks or magazines by your bedside.** "What? You must be joking." No, I'm dead serious! When you're settling down for the day and ready to nod off to sleep, take a tour through a food magazine or cookbook – you'll be pleasantly surprised how inspired you can become from reading about food and recipes.

- **Cook with a friend or partner.** Share it all – from deciding what to eat, planning the menu, doing the shopping, cooking, and clean up.

- **Better yet, cook with your children, your friends' children, or your grandchildren.** Pass on your knowledge, your interests, your spirit, and your passion for food. At the same time, you'll be passing on your values that cooking is something worth doing.

'Da-mental' in fun'damentals' – the top 10 'must know' **Nutrition** facts:

- **If the food doesn't taste good, you probably won't eat it,** no matter how nutritious it is for you. So work at finding foods and flavours you love.

- **Let common sense prevail** – if the nutrition claim for a food or dietary regime sounds too good to be true, it probably isn't going to do what it says. Look for proof, and if proof isn't available, above all, let common sense prevail.

- **Keep it simple – the tried and true messages of 'variety' and 'moderation' have stood the test of time.** Eating habits that include lots of different foods ensure you get the variety of the nutrients that you need every day. Moderation basically means to have a little bit of everything you like. Even if it's chocolate cake, cheesecake, or foie gras, have a little bit and enjoy it!

- **Be mindful of fat.** Fats are found

  ~ naturally in dairy products, meat products, nuts, and seeds

  ~ naturally in oils (mostly derived from nuts and seeds – such as sunflower, peanut, etc)

  ~ added to products such as cookies, cakes, crackers, donuts, and other bread and pastry products.

  When watching the amount of fat you eat, be mindful of both the **amount** and **type** of fat you choose.

  To reduce the **amount** of fat you eat, choose lower fat dairy products and select lean meats [those that have little visible fat and those that have little marbling (fat that runs through the meat)]. Skip the donut or croissant and opt for a lower fat bread choice such as whole grain bread or a bagel. To make wise fat choices with the **type** of fat, choose fats most often that are liquid at room temperature such as olive, canola, grapeseed, peanut, sunflower, and safflower oils. Again, let the voice of moderation guide you.

- **Pick a pretty plate!** Go for fruits and vegetables that are deeply coloured with red, orange, and green. There's great nutrition in those foods that are rich in colour. Reach for reds like red peppers and tomatoes, forage for orange like oranges, squashes, sweet potatoes, and mangoes, and go for greens like broccoli and spinach. And don't forget about one of the only naturally occurring blue foods – the delicious blueberry – so small, sweet, richly coloured, and bursting with nutrition.

- **Keep all food safe to eat.** When cooking, follow the simple principle of 'keep hot foods hot' and 'keep cold foods cold'. Hot foods should be kept above 140°F (60°C) and cold foods kept below 40°F (4°C). Harmful bacteria can grow when protein-based foods like eggs, mayonnaise, chicken, and beef are left at temperatures between 40°F (4°C) and140°F (60°C). So, don't invite any unwanted germs to your party. Follow safe principles for handling food. For more information, check out: www.cfia.ca.

- **Balancing the scales.** There's nothing magic about weight control. For most people, it's simply a question of balance – if you eat more energy in the form of food than you use in the form of physical activity, you will likely gain weight. The opposite is also true – if you eat less energy in the form of food than you use in the form of physical activity, you will likely lose weight. So, if you're out to shed a few pounds, the bottom line message is eat less and move more. If you need help figuring out the perfect balance for you, contact a Registered Dietitian. You can also visit reputable web sites for information such as www.dietitians.ca for helpful tips.

- **Special needs at special times.** There may be times during your life when you need to watch what you eat a little more closely – when you're pregnant or have other special nutritional needs to help with an acute or chronic disease. Be sure you speak with your doctor about your needs. Then seek the help of a Registered Dietitian to get you through these special times. Check out www.dietitians.ca to find a dietitian in your area.

- **Salt, alcohol, and caffeine.** Practice moderation when it comes to components like salt, alcohol, and caffeine. They add variety and interest to your diet and can be enjoyed occasionally.

- **Enjoy what you eat!** Healthy eating is delicious, and provides a range of tastes, colours, and textures. Enjoy foods from your own heritage and try those from other cultures.

'Da-mental' in fun'damentals' – the top 10 'must know' **cooking** facts:

- **Organize your kitchen** – There's no one way to organize a kitchen, and you need to do what works best for you. A little planning at the outset goes a long way to save you time and frustration. Find a good home for pots, pans, cooking and baking utensils, and ingredients. Maybe you like all your tools visible and want to put them in containers on the counters? Maybe you like everything put away in drawers? Do what works best for you so that when you're ready to cook, it's a pleasure and not a pain.

- **Knives and pots** – Do your homework and invest wisely. Good pots and knives can last a lifetime, or you could be replacing them often if the quality is poor. Talk with chefs, watch cooking shows, take a class at a local culinary school, and research the Internet.

- **Recipes** – If a recipe name catches your eye, read on. Before you start to prepare any recipe, read it from start to finish – do you know what you're in for? do you have all the skills, time, tools, and ingredients that you need? does the recipe make sense? does it sound tasty or do the flavours fight with each other? do you need to buy specialty ingredients that you may only need to use this once and then have it collect dust on your shelves? Experiment with recipes. Funny as it sounds, not all recipes work! Not that any author purposely intends to deceive you, but all sorts of variables can affect the success of a recipe: climate, altitude, and technique can all affect the outcome. The only way to know is to try.

- **Ingredients** – Have staples on hand so that you can prepare everyday meals. Staples include a variety of fresh, canned, and frozen foods that can be used in everyday cooking. For a list of staples for you to consider, check out www.dietitians.ca and take the Virtual Grocery Store Tour (under 'Eat Well, Live Well'). For specialty recipes, buy the right type and amount of ingredient for the recipe. Look for value for your dollar and buy only what you need and can reasonably use before it turns to 'funny green stuff' in your fridge.

- **Mise en Place** – that's chef talk for 'have everything in its place before you start'. This means having the bread baking pan ready to put the bread in after you've made it; it also means having your fresh ingredients cut, your canned goods opened, your frozen foods defrosted, and all your tools ready to go BEFORE you start to cook. We've all done it – gotten to the middle of a recipe and said, 'Uh-oh, I'm out of baking powder, now what?' Mise en place means that you've done your homework and everything you need to make the recipe is at hand and ready to use.

- **Heat and Meat – Friend or Foe?** Generally speaking, the most expensive ingredients you'll cook with are meat products including beef, pork, lamb, fish, shellfish, and poultry. When you've invested good money in these items, you don't want to ruin them – you want them to taste perfect. So, get familiar with heat, how it works, and what type of heat is best for the item you're cooking. Here are a few basics:

    ~ Meat is composed of primarily protein. When you add heat and 'cook' protein, the fibres in the meat become firm. The cut of meat you have will determine the best type of heat to use to cook the product.

    ~ There are two ways to cook with heat: **dry heat** and **moist heat**.

    Dry heat cooking methods are when the heat comes into direct contact with the food. This includes methods such as broiling, grilling, roasting, sautéing, and pan-frying. The best cuts of meat for this type of cooking include the tender cuts that have enough fat in them so that the fat melts when it comes into contact with the heat and helps to make a juicy product. For beef, this means grilling or broiling cuts such as sirloin or rib eye steaks or roasting prime rib. The same goes for pork and lamb. Most poultry, fish, and shellfish can be cooked using dry heat methods, but the key is not to overcook. We've all had dried out, overcooked chicken breast, turkey, and fish, or rubbery shrimp. Experience and following recipes will help you determine when items cooked in dry heat are cooked well enough to be safe and tasty, but not overcooked.

    Moist heat cooking methods are when both heat and moisture are applied to the meat. Moist heat is often used to tenderize cuts of meat through long, slow cooking and exposure to moisture. Tough cuts of meat like blade roasts, brisket, stew meat, etc. need extra cooking care to tenderize them. The long, slow cooking process breaks down the tough fibres in the meat, known as connective tissue and collagen, producing a mouth-watering end product. Pot roasts, stews, and boiled dinners that start with tough cuts of meat are all delicious products of moist heat. So, pick your heat wisely and use the right type of cooking method to match the cut of meat you're preparing.

- **Soggy, Limp Vegetables No More!** Here again, heat can be our friend or foe. Thankfully, gone are the days of overcooked, soggy, limp vegetables. The fresh taste of fresh and frozen vegetables can be retained by choosing the right cooking method. Great ways to cook vegetables include steaming, sautéing, and stir-frying where the colour, crunch, and flavour of the vegetable are retained.

- **Flavours that work** – So, just how do you know that ginger is a delightful flavour accompaniment to carrots, or that chocolate and raspberries were destined to be married? But carrots and cranberry juice, or chocolate and wasabi? These combinations just sound awful! There's an entire science devoted to taste and flavour, and without getting too technical, it's all about getting to know food, the flavours of food, and what combinations work to enhance or complement each other. The best way to know what flavours work for you is to be brave and experiment. Read the recipe and imagine the taste.

- **Baking is a different kettle of fish than cooking!** There are indeed some basic principles in cooking, but after time, many people don't even use recipes – they go with the basic principles of cooking and use the foods they like to create the flavours they want. Not so with baking. Baking is indeed much more of a precise effort and relies on chemistry principles. Tinkering with ingredients of leavened bread recipes can result in unleavened bread; playing with baking soda or baking powder in muffins, biscuits, or cakes can leave you with bitter products; forgetting to whip the egg whites in angel food cake will give you an egg white omelette! And on it goes – the lesson here is not to mess with recipes of baked products. Sure, you can add a few nuts to some chocolate chip cookies and not damage the end product, but all in all, it's best to follow recipes for baked items.

- **Play with your food!** Cooking for me is a lot like playing at the park. I get the chance to meet new ingredients, try new toys, and at the end of the day, feel satisfied that I've had a great new experience. Go ahead, get back into the kitchen – it's a great gathering place to learn and to have fun!

FLAVOURFUL MENUS

To make your life simple and your meal memorable and full of flavour, here are a few sample menus for everyday use and for special occasions.

Gourmet Dinner

Friday Night Supper

Harvest Moon Supper

Winter Weekend Supper

BREAKFAST – TO BREAK THE FAST

There's a reason why the first meal of the day is called breakfast, as it literally means to 'break the fast' and nourish your body after being deprived of energy during sleep.

The value of breakfast cannot be overstated. Wise words have been handed down for centuries to eat breakfast – all for very good reasons. We know that breakfast-eating children and teenagers perform better in school, and breakfast-eating adults are clearer in their thinking. We also know that breakfast eaters have an easier time controlling their weight as they are less likely to binge on a larger meal at lunchtime.

A healthy and tasty breakfast can be very simple – a bowl of whole-grain cereal with lower fat milk and a piece of fresh fruit are all it takes to get a healthy breakfast. Ideally, a healthy breakfast includes foods from three of the four food groups, always including a good source of protein such as milk, yogurt, egg, meat, cheese, or peanut butter. Protein helps to give us 'staying power' through the morning. It also gives our bodies essential nutrients to repair worn-out cells and body tissues and to build any needed new ones.

Despite the simplicity of a healthy breakfast, we've all faced challenges getting nourishment at this very busy time of the day. A few helpful tips include:

- Plan ahead for breakfast – perhaps even set out the bowl and cereal box the night before to remind you to eat.
- Make items ahead of time – all of the muffin and scone recipes that follow freeze very well. Simply freeze them individually and then pull them out of the freezer before you step in the shower.
- Pack a lunch tote with a freezer pack and fill it with snack-happy items such as yogurt, fresh fruit, muffins, cheese, juice boxes, or granola bars.
- Try different smoothie flavours – a quick whirl in a blender can give you a delicious and healthy start to your day.
- Try some of the recipes that follow and enjoy a healthy and delicious start to your day!

MAKING MARVELLOUS MUFFINS

There's nothing like a warm, fresh, homemade muffin! The 'muffin method' will produce a delightful product that is tender, dense, and moist in texture, even in shape, and full of flavour. The muffin method is simple: stir the dry ingredients together in one bowl, the wet ingredients in another bowl, and then add the liquid ingredients to the dry and stir just until the ingredients are combined. Over mixing the ingredients is the most common mistake and produces a less tender muffin with occasional coarse 'tunnels' – elongated holes which form when the overly mixed batter traps the leavening gas in large pockets.

Muffins are best eaten on the day they are made because they stale quickly. This happens because the small amount of mixing doesn't allow the fat to disperse enough to keep the starch moist. Besides, the well-made, tasty muffins that follow won't last past a day anyway! All of the following muffin recipes freeze well.

1. Nutrition Note:

   Muffins can often be higher in fat than we like. For a lower fat muffin, check that the amount of fat (butter, margarine, oil, or shortening) is no greater than 1/4-1/3 cup (60-75 mL) for a dozen muffins. As well, watch for higher fat ingredients such as added cheese, sour cream, or chocolate.

   You can also change your favourite higher fat muffin recipe to a lower fat recipe using one of the following ideas:

   - Substitute half of the fat with an equal amount of pureed fruit such as applesauce, carrots, prunes, etc. For example, if a banana muffin recipe calls for 2/3 cup (150 mL) oil, use 1/3 cup (75 mL) oil and 1/3 cup (75 mL) applesauce.

   - If a recipe calls for whole milk, use 1% or skim milk instead.

   - If a recipe calls for cheese, use a lower fat cheese or reduce the cheese by half.

   - If a recipe calls for buttermilk, use 1% instead of 3.25% MF buttermilk.

   - If a recipe calls for sour cream, use lower fat sour cream or plain low fat yogurt.

2. Baking Note: Here's a simple lesson in flours:

   Wheat flour is the finely sifted and ground meal of the wheat kernel. Flour is milled from either hard wheat, which is high in gluten (the protein that allows bread to trap gases when it rises), or soft wheat, which is lower in gluten. There are three parts to the wheat kernel: the bran, or outer coating, contains fibre, B vitamins, and several minerals; the next layer is the germ, which provides more B vitamins and a small amount of fat; the endosperm is the innermost layer, which provides protein, carbohydrate, and B vitamins.

   Whole wheat flour is milled using all three components. It's higher in fibre and most nutrients than most other flours, and because it contains some fat, it should be stored in the refrigerator if not used quickly.

   All-purpose flour is very refined and is made by milling only the endosperm of a combination of hard and soft wheats. Since the bran has been stripped away in processing, it contains virtually no fibre. Because the germ was not used in processing, most flours are enriched – meaning that the nutrients lost in processing are added back to the flour. This is the most common type of flour used in general baking of cookies, quick breads, squares, etc.

   Cake or pastry flour is made from soft wheat and has a very fine texture suitable for baking delicate cakes and pastries.

   In recipes for muffins, cookies, quick breads, and other not-so-delicate items, up to half of the all-purpose flour can be substituted with whole wheat flour without any significant effect on the product. Products that are made exclusively with whole wheat flour tend to be nuttier and slightly sweeter in flavour, more dense in texture, and brown-flecked in colour.

BANANA CHOCOLATE CHIP MUFFINS

What better combination of flavours than banana and chocolate! These can be an occasional treat for the kids for breakfast or after school, and they're also a nice addition to a brunch table.

Bananas are loved by most everyone and are an excellent source of potassium. You can also eliminate the chocolate chips and replace them with an equal amount of dried fruit or nuts of your choice. The oats add a delightful texture. This recipe makes 2 dozen muffins so it's a good recipe to use if you need to take muffins to a school or work function. The recipe can also be cut in half if you prefer.

1/3 cup (75 mL) vegetable oil

1 cup (250 mL) white sugar

2 large eggs

1 1/2 teaspoons (7.5 mL) vanilla extract

5 medium overripe bananas,
mashed with a fork in a small bowl

1/2 cup (125 mL) semisweet chocolate chips

1/2 cup (125 mL) unsweetened applesauce

2 cups (500 mL) all-purpose flour

2 teaspoons (10 mL) baking powder

2 teaspoons (10 mL) baking soda

2 cups (500 mL) large flake oats

1. Preheat oven to 400°F (200°C). Line 24 muffin tins with paper liners.

2. In a medium mixing bowl, mix oil and sugar until well blended. Add eggs, vanilla, bananas, chocolate chips, and applesauce. Stir to combine.

3. In a separate mixing bowl, combine flour, oats, baking powder, and baking soda.

4. Add egg mixture to the dry ingredients and stir to combine.

5. Scoop batter into prepared paper-lined cups, filling 2/3 full. Bake for 18-20 minutes or until muffins spring back when lightly touched.

Makes: 24 muffins

CHEESY JALAPENO CORNMEAL MUFFINS

Corn is a gift to us from Native Americans and dates back nearly 7,000 years. Cornmeal is made by grinding corn kernels into one of three textures: fine, medium, or coarse, and is either yellow, white, or blue depending on the type of corn used. Cornmeal is typically used in making cornbread and Hush Puppies, a Southern specialty cornmeal dumpling. Legend has it that the name comes from tossing scraps of the dumpling to hungry dogs to keep them from begging for food, saying, 'hush, puppy'.

Here, cornmeal adds a wonderful grainy texture to these muffins. They can take on quite a spicy flavour if you use all the cayenne and jalapeno peppers. They also make a nice accompaniment to chilli or soup.

1 cup (250 mL) yellow cornmeal

1 cup (250 mL) all-purpose flour

1 tablespoon (15 mL) baking powder

1 teaspoon (5 mL) salt

1/2 teaspoon (2.5 mL) baking soda

1/4 teaspoon (1.25 mL) cayenne pepper

1/2 cup (125 mL) canned kernel corn, drained

1 tablespoon (15 mL) finely chopped jalapeno pepper (optional)

1 cup (250 mL) grated aged Cheddar cheese

1 cup (250 mL) buttermilk (3.25% or 1% MF)

1/2 cup (125 mL) melted butter

1 large egg

1. Preheat oven to 425°F (215°C). Line 12 muffin cups with paper liners.

2. In a large mixing bowl, combine cornmeal, flour, baking powder, salt, baking soda, and cayenne pepper. Mix well. Stir in corn, jalapeno pepper, and grated cheese.

3. In small bowl, combine buttermilk, melted butter, and egg and then add to dry ingredients. Stir just to combine; do not over mix.

4. Fill prepared paper-lined cups 2/3 full. Bake for 18-20 minutes or until muffins spring back when touched.

Makes: 12 muffins

HAM AND CHEESE MUFFINS

Many years ago, my dear friend Kathy and I stopped at a local muffin shop and tried a delicious Ham and Cheese Muffin. We promptly asked the pastry chef at work to try and recreate them. After many attempts, we had success! These work best if you use a non-stick muffin pan, or if using paper muffin cups, spray them with a non-stick cooking spray to prevent sticking. They have a dense texture as opposed to a light muffin. They are ideal for a morning snack, for lunch with yogurt and some fresh fruit, and they make a nice addition to a breakfast buffet table.

1/2 cup (125 mL) vegetable oil

3 tablespoons (45 mL) white sugar

2 large eggs

4 cups (1 L) all-purpose flour

1 tablespoon (15 mL) baking powder

1/4 teaspoon (1.25 mL) salt

1 3/4 cups (425 mL) 2% milk

1 cup (250 mL) grated medium Cheddar cheese

3/4 cup (175 mL) finely chopped deli-style ham, such as Black Forest

1. Preheat oven to 400°F (200°C). Line 20 muffin cups with paper liners and spray with non-stick cooking spray.

2. In a mixing bowl, beat oil and sugar together until well combined. Add eggs and blend well.

3. In a separate mixing bowl, combine flour, baking powder, and salt. Add dry ingredients alternately with milk to egg mixture, stirring with each addition just enough to combine. Add cheese and diced ham. Stir to combine.

4. Scoop batter into prepared paper-lined and greased cups, filling 2/3 full. Bake for 25-30 minutes until muffins spring back when touched.

Tasting Note: You can vary the cheese to your taste preference. Try using Monterey Jack or Asiago for variety. You can also vary the ham by replacing it with a spicy salami. This recipe can be cut in half if you want to make fewer muffins.

Makes: 20 muffins

ORANGE MARMALADE DATE MUFFINS

This flavour combination is one of my favourites – the sweetness of the dates and the tartness of the oranges work great together. The 'whole' orange is used for full flavour.

Marmalade is a preserve that contains pieces of fruit rind, generally citrus fruit, so these muffins are aptly named. They're moist and tangy and rich in Vitamin C.

1 medium whole orange (including rind), washed and cut into quarters; seeds and tough white membrane removed

1/2 cup (125 mL) orange juice (in addition to whole orange above)

1/2 cup (125 mL) chopped, pitted dates

1 teaspoon (5 mL) baking soda

1 1/2 cups (375 mL) all-purpose flour

1 teaspoon (5 mL) baking powder

1 teaspoon (5 mL) salt

1 large egg

1/2 cup (125 mL) soft butter

3/4 cup (175 mL) brown sugar

1. Preheat oven to 400°F (200°C). Line 12 muffin cups with paper liners.

2. Place quartered orange and orange juice in blender or food processor, and whirl until finely chopped. Transfer to a small saucepan and add dates and baking soda. Heat mixture on stovetop to a boil and then simmer for 5 minutes to allow dates to soften; stir occasionally to prevent burning. Remove from heat and set aside to cool for 10 minutes.

3. In a medium mixing bowl, combine flour, baking powder, and salt. Stir to combine.

4. In a medium mixing bowl, cream egg, butter, and brown sugar until well combined. Add cooled orange/date mixture. Stir to combine.

5. Add wet ingredients to dry ingredients and stir only until combined; do not over mix.

6. Fill prepared paper-lined cups 2/3 full. Bake for about 15-18 minutes or until muffins spring back when touched.

Makes: 12 muffins

PINEAPPLE BRAN MUFFINS

Many bran muffin recipes can be dry. This recipe is full of the goodness of a whole grain cereal, and the added pineapple and buttermilk keep it moist.

2 cups (500 mL) All Bran® original cereal
1 cup (250 mL) buttermilk (3.25% or 1% MF)
1/2 cup (125 mL) white sugar
1/3 cup (75 mL) whole wheat flour
3/4 cup (175 mL) all-purpose flour
1/4 teaspoon (1.25 mL) salt
1/2 teaspoon (2.5 mL) baking soda
1/2 teaspoon (2.5 mL) baking powder
3/4 teaspoon (3.75 mL) ground cinnamon
2 large eggs
2 tablespoons (30 mL) honey
2 tablespoons (30 mL) vegetable oil
1/2 cup (125 mL) crushed pineapple, drained

1. Preheat oven to 400°F (200°C). Line 12 muffin cups with paper liners.

2. In a medium size bowl, mix All Bran® original cereal with buttermilk. Stir to combine and let soak for 10-15 minutes.

3. In another mixing bowl, combine sugar, whole wheat flour, all-purpose flour, salt, baking soda, baking powder, and cinnamon.

4. In a small bowl, combine eggs, honey, oil, and pineapple. Stir to combine. Add to softened cereal and buttermilk mixture and stir.

5. Add wet ingredients to dry ingredients and stir only to combine.

6. Fill prepared paper-lined cups 2/3 full. Bake for 16-18 minutes or until muffins spring back when touched.

Makes: 12 muffins

SWEET POTATO PECAN MUFFINS

The dark orange colour of pureed sweet potatoes yields a rich-coloured muffin that's loaded with nutrition. Since the potatoes are so moist, there is little additional fat needed. Toasting the pecans gives them a more intense flavour. To toast pecans, preheat the oven to 350°F (180°C). Place pecans on baking sheet, being careful to space them out so they are all on one layer. Toast in the oven for 5-7 minutes, or until they start to darken. Watch them carefully as they can quickly burn.

1 cup (250 mL) cooked, mashed sweet potatoes
2 large eggs
1/2 cup (125 mL) white sugar
1/3 cup (75 mL) brown sugar
1/2 cup (125 mL) 2% milk
1 cup (250 mL) all-purpose flour
1 cup (250 mL) whole wheat flour
1 1/2 teaspoons (7.5 mL) baking soda
2 tablespoons (30 mL) baking powder
1 teaspoon (5 mL) salt
1 teaspoon (5 mL) ground cinnamon
1 teaspoon (5 mL) ground nutmeg
1 cup (250 mL) coarsely chopped toasted pecans

1. Preheat oven to 350°F (180°C). Line 12 muffin cups with paper liners.

2. In a medium mixing bowl, combine sweet potatoes, eggs, sugars, and milk. Stir to combine.

3. In a separate mixing bowl, combine flours, baking soda, baking powder, salt, and spices. Add wet ingredients to dry ingredients. Stir to combine. Do not over mix. Stir in toasted pecans.

4. Scoop batter into prepared paper-lined cups filling 2/3 full and bake for 18-20 minutes or until muffins spring back when touched.

Makes: 12 muffins

WILD BLUEBERRY MUFFINS WITH STREUSEL TOPPING

Wild blueberries are readily available frozen in most supermarkets. They tend to be smaller than the regular blueberry and have more intense flavour. If wild blueberries are not available, substitute regular fresh or frozen blueberries.

1/3 cup (75 mL) vegetable oil

3/4 cup (175 mL) white sugar

2 large eggs

1 teaspoon (5 mL) vanilla extract

1 1/2 cups (375 mL) all-purpose flour

3/4 teaspoon (3.75 mL) baking powder

3/4 teaspoon (3.75 mL) baking soda

1/2 teaspoon (2.5 mL) salt

1/2 cup (125 mL) regular or fat-reduced sour cream

3/4 cup (190 mL) frozen wild blueberries
(or fresh, if available)

1. Preheat oven to 375°F (190°C). Line 12 muffin cups with paper liners.

2. In a medium mixing bowl, combine oil and sugar and mix well. Beat in eggs and mix well. Stir in vanilla extract.

3. In a separate mixing bowl, stir together flour, baking powder, baking soda, and salt. Add wet ingredients to dry ingredients alternately with sour cream, stirring after each addition. Gently fold in blueberries.

4. Spoon batter into prepared paper-lined cups, filling 2/3 full. Sprinkle each with Streusel Topping. Bake for 18-20 minutes or until muffins spring back when touched.

Continued...

WILD BLUEBERRY MUFFINS WITH STREUSEL TOPPING
continued...

Streusel Topping:

1 tablespoon (15 mL) soft butter

1/4 teaspoon (1.25 mL) ground cinnamon

1/4 cup (60 mL) all-purpose flour

1/3 cup (75 mL) white sugar

1. In a small mixing bowl, combine all ingredients with a spoon or your fingertips.
2. Evenly distribute over muffins before baking.

Makes: 12 muffins

MAKING PERFECT SCONES

The key to a perfect scone is all in the hands. Over-mixing will give you a tough and dry product. To get a flaky, moist scone, once the dry ingredients have been mixed, cut the butter in only until it forms meal the size of peas. When adding the wet ingredient, mix gently with a spoon or by hand and only until the mixture starts to hold together. Turn the dough out onto a lightly floured work surface, knead it only 4-5 times and pat it out gently to a uniform size. Don't be disheartened if it takes a few times making the recipe to get a tender product-it's all in the hands and takes time to get the ideal texture. Scones are delicious for breakfast served with fresh fruit, fruit compotes, or flavoured butters. You'll be the hit of the office if you bring the White Chocolate and Blueberry Scones to the next meeting!

CHEDDAR CHEESE SCONES

Aged Cheddar cheese works best in these scones. You can also use Applewood Smoked Cheddar to give a smoky flavour.

2 1/4 cups (560 mL) all-purpose flour

1 tablespoon (15 mL) baking powder

1/2 teaspoon (2.5 mL) baking soda

1/2 teaspoon (2.5 mL) salt

1/2-1 teaspoon (2.5-5 mL) cayenne pepper, depending on preferred taste

1/2 cup (125 mL) COLD butter

1 cup (250 mL) grated aged Cheddar cheese

1 cup (250 mL) buttermilk (3.25% or 1% MF)

Optional Egg Wash: 1 egg, lightly whisked and mixed with 1 teaspoon (5 mL) whipping cream and dash salt (this gives a nice gloss to the top)

1. Preheat oven to 425°F (215°C). Lightly grease a large baking sheet or line with parchment paper.
2. Sift flour, baking powder, baking soda, salt, and cayenne pepper into a large mixing bowl. Cut in cold butter with a pastry cutter or two butter knives until the size of peas. Stir in Cheddar cheese.
3. Add buttermilk and stir gently with a wooden spoon until most of the liquid is incorporated.
4. Turn mixture out onto lightly floured work surface and knead 4-5 times to finish incorporating.
5. Pat mixture out to 3/4 inch (1.5 cm) thickness. Cut out scones with 2 inch (5 cm) biscuit cutter. Place on prepared baking sheet. If using Egg Wash, brush scones liberally. Bake for 12-14 minutes until the tops are golden brown. Remove to cooling rack until ready to eat. These scones also freeze beautifully.

Makes: 12 scones

HARVEST PUMPKIN SCONES

The beautiful pumpkin is a member of the gourd family, which also includes muskmelon and squash, and, surprisingly, the watermelon. The Native Indians of North America were using pumpkins when the colonists landed. They soon embraced the many uses of this versatile fruit, the most popular of which is the traditional Pumpkin Pie which graces nearly every table at North American Thanksgiving feasts. This beta-carotene rich fruit is easily available year round in canned form, and it often takes centre stage in soups, muffins, and breads. Here it is combined with sweet spices, buttermilk, and pecans for a truly special scone.

1 cup (250 mL) all-purpose flour

3/4 cup (175 mL) whole wheat flour

1/2 cup (125 mL) white sugar

1 tablespoon (15 mL) baking powder

1/2 teaspoon (2.5 mL) baking soda

1/4 teaspoon (1.25 mL) salt

1/2 teaspoon (2.5 mL) EACH ground cinnamon and nutmeg

1/4 teaspoon (1.25 mL) ground cloves

1/2 cup (125 mL) COLD butter

1/2 cup (125 mL) canned pumpkin

1/2 cup (125 mL) buttermilk (3.25% or 1% MF)

1/3 cup (75 mL) chopped pecans

1 tablespoon (15 mL) coarse brown sugar

1. Preheat oven to 375°F (190°C). Lightly grease a large baking sheet or line with parchment paper.

2. In a large mixing bowl, combine flours, sugar, baking powder, baking soda, salt, and spices. Stir to combine. Cut in cold butter with a pastry cutter or two butter knives until the size of peas.

3. In a small bowl, stir together pumpkin and buttermilk. Add to dry ingredients and stir just until moistened. Fold in nuts.

4. Transfer dough to prepared baking sheet. Using floured hands, pat dough to 8 inch (20 cm) circle. Using a long knife, score dough into 8 wedges, but do not separate. Sprinkle dough with brown sugar. Bake for 20-25 minutes or until top springs back when lightly touched. Cool slightly and cut again into wedges.

Makes: 8 large scones

WHITE CHOCOLATE AND BLUEBERRY SCONES

Of all the scone variations I've made, this is a winning combination. Other optional sweet variations include:
1 cup (250 mL) raisins
or
1 cup (250 mL) dried cranberries and 1 tablespoon (15 mL) grated lemon zest
or
1 cup (250 mL) finely chopped dried apricots
or
1/4 cup (60 mL) chopped candied ginger
or
2/3 cup (150 mL) chopped dried dates and 1 tablespoon (15 mL) grated orange zest

2 1/4 cups (560 mL) all-purpose flour

1/3 cup (75 mL) white sugar

1 tablespoon (15 mL) baking powder

1/2 teaspoon (2.5 mL) baking soda

1/2 teaspoon (2.5 mL) salt

1/2 cup (125 mL) COLD butter

1 cup (250 mL) buttermilk (3.25% or 1% MF)

Optional Egg Wash: 1 large egg whisked with
1 teaspoon (5 mL) whipping cream and a dash of salt

1/2 cup (125 mL) frozen blueberries and
1/2 cup (125 mL) chopped white chocolate

1. Preheat oven to 425°F (215°C). Lightly grease a large baking sheet or line with parchment paper.

2. In large mixing bowl, combine flour, sugar, baking powder, baking soda, and salt. Cut in cold butter with a pastry cutter or two butter knives until the size of peas. Fold in frozen blueberries and white chocolate.

3. Add buttermilk and stir gently with a wooden spoon until most of the liquid is incorporated.

4. Turn mixture out onto lightly floured work surface and knead 4-5 times to incorporate remaining dry ingredients. Pat mixture out to 3/4 inch (1.5 cm) thickness. Cut with a 2 inch (5 cm) biscuit cutter.

5. Place on prepared baking sheet. Brush with egg wash (if desired) and sprinkle with coarse sugar (if desired). Bake for 12-14 minutes until the tops are very light golden brown.

6. Remove to cooling rack until ready to eat. These scones also freeze beautifully.

Makes: 12 scones

PEPPERED BACON SCONES WITH MAPLE BUTTER

The cornmeal in these scones gives them a unique but delightful texture that complements the bacon.

2 cups (500 mL) all-purpose flour

2 tablespoons (30 mL) white sugar

1 tablespoon (15 mL) baking powder

1/2 teaspoon (2.5 mL) salt

1/2 teaspoon (2.5 mL) baking soda

1/4 cup (60 mL) yellow cornmeal

1/2 teaspoon (2.5 mL) freshly ground black pepper

1/2 cup (125 mL) COLD butter

8 pepper-crusted bacon slices, cooked until crisp and crumbled (if you can't find pepper-crusted bacon, use regular bacon)

1 cup (250 mL) buttermilk (3.25 or 1% MF)

1. Preheat oven to 425°F (215°C). Lightly grease a large baking sheet.

2. In a large mixing bowl, stir together flour, sugar, baking powder, salt, baking soda, cornmeal, and black pepper. Cut in cold butter with a pastry blender or two butter knives until small pea-size pieces of fat remain. Stir in bacon.

3. Add buttermilk and stir gently with a wooden spoon until most of the liquid is incorporated.

4. Turn mixture out onto lightly floured work surface and knead 4-5 times to finish incorporating.

5. Pat mixture to 3/4 inch (1.5 cm). Cut out scones with 2 inch (5 cm) biscuit cutter. Place on baking sheet. Bake for 12-14 minutes.

6. Serve with Maple Butter.

Makes: 12 scones

Continued...

PEPPERED BACON SCONES WITH MAPLE BUTTER

continued...

Maple Butter:

1/2 cup (125 mL) softened butter

2 tablespoons (30 mL) pure maple syrup

1. In a small mixing bowl, place butter and syrup. Mix with electric mixture until syrup is fully incorporated.

2. Form into 1 inch (2.5 cm) wide log and wrap in plastic wrap until firm. Slice into discs and serve with scones.

Makes: 1/2 cup (125 mL)

WHOLE WHEAT, DATE, ORANGE, AND GINGER SCONES

The use of whole wheat flour here gives a nice nutty complementary flavour to the sweet dates, orange and ginger.

2 cups (500 mL) whole wheat flour
1 tablespoon (15 mL) baking powder
1/2 teaspoon (2.5 mL) baking soda
1/2 teaspoon (2.5 mL) salt
1/2 cup (125 mL) COLD butter
1/2 cup (125 mL) finely chopped pitted dates
1 tablespoon (15 mL) finely grated orange zest
2 teaspoons (30 mL) finely chopped, candied ginger
1 large egg, lightly whisked
3 tablespoons (45 mL) honey
1/4 cup (60 mL) orange juice
1/2 cup (125 mL) buttermilk (3.25% or 1% MF)

1. Preheat oven to 400°F (200°C). Lightly grease a large baking sheet or line with parchment paper.
2. Sift flours, baking powder, baking soda, and salt into a large mixing bowl. Cut in cold butter with a pastry cutter or two butter knives until the size of peas. Stir in chopped dates, orange zest, and candied ginger.
3. In a small mixing bowl, combine egg, honey, orange juice, and buttermilk. Stir gently to combine. Add to dry ingredients and stir gently with a wooden spoon until most of the liquid is incorporated.
4. Turn mixture out on to lightly floured work surface and knead 4-5 times to incorporate all ingredients.
5. Pat mixture to 3/4 inch (1.5 cm) thick. Cut out scones with 2 inch (5 cm) biscuit cutter. Place on prepared baking sheets and bake for 12-14 minutes until the tops are lightly golden brown.
6. Remove to cooling racks.

Makes: 12 scones

Ham and Cheese Muffins
page 6

Whole Grain Bread with Oats, Flax, and Millet

page 28

EGGS CODDLED IN TOMATOES, ONIONS, AND PEPPERS

This dish is perfect for a brunch table. For each serving, scoop out one egg and some tomato mixture and serve on a toasted English muffin or sourdough bread slice.

2 tablespoons (30 mL) olive oil

1 EACH yellow and red pepper, stems and seeds removed, thinly sliced

1 jalapeno pepper, stem and seeds removed and finely chopped

2 medium onions, thinly sliced

2 garlic cloves, finely minced

19-ounce (540 mL) can diced tomatoes with juice

2 teaspoons (10 mL) chilli powder

2 teaspoons (10 mL) dried oregano

1/2 teaspoon (2.5 mL) salt

1 teaspoon (5 mL) freshly ground black pepper

6 large eggs

1 cup (250 mL) grated Gruyere or Monterey Jack cheese

1. Preheat oven to 400°F (200°C).

2. In a medium skillet, heat olive oil over medium-high heat. Add peppers, jalapeno pepper, onions, and garlic. Cook until onions and peppers begin to soften, about 5-7 minutes. Add tomatoes, spices, salt, and pepper. Bring to a boil; reduce heat and simmer for about 15-20 minutes until thick and only a small amount of liquid remains. Remove from heat.

3. Place tomato mixture in lightly greased 9 inch (23 cm) round or square baking pan. Form 6 'holes' for eggs. Break eggs into holes. Cover mixture evenly with grated cheese. Bake, uncovered, about 15 minutes until eggs are set and cheese is melted.

Serves: 6

FARMER'S FRITTATA

A frittata is basically an open-faced omelette with generous amounts of hearty ingredients. They can be made in small pans for individual servings, or made for a family in a large, oven-proof skillet and then cut into individual wedges. The frittata is first cooked on the stove and then finished under the broiler. This frittata is a great way to use up extra baked potatoes!

3 tablespoons (45 mL) olive oil

1 cup (250 mL) finely diced white or yellow onion

2 garlic cloves, finely minced

2 medium baked russet potatoes (skins left on or off), roughly cut into 1/2 inch (1 cm) cubes [about 1 cup (250 mL) cubed potatoes]

1 red bell pepper, stem and seeds removed, coarsely chopped

8 large eggs, whisked in a small bowl with salt and freshly ground black pepper, to taste

1/4 cup (60 mL) freshly grated Parmesan cheese

1/2 cup (125 mL) grated old Cheddar cheese

1. Preheat broiler to low.
2. Heat 1 tablespoon (15 mL) olive oil in 10 inch (25 cm) cast iron or other oven proof skillet. Add onions and cook on medium-high heat for 3-5 minutes until onions are wilted but not browned. Add garlic and cook 1 minute more. Remove from pan and set aside.
3. Heat remaining oil in skillet. Add potatoes and peppers. Cook on medium heat for 8-10 minutes or until peppers are soft and potatoes are heated through. Return onions and garlic to pan with peppers and potatoes.
4. Pour eggs over mixture. Stir to combine. Cook for 3-5 minutes, gently lifting cooked edge with a spatula so the uncooked portion can flow to the bottom. Cook until eggs are nearly set but still moist on top. Remove from heat.
5. Sprinkle cheeses evenly over eggs. Place skillet under preheated broiler and broil 1-2 minutes to melt cheeses. Remove from broiler.
6. Place one or two large spatulas under the frittata and carefully remove to a serving plate.

Serves: 4-6

HAM AND CHEESE FRITTATA WITH GREEN ONIONS AND FRESH APPLES

The apple and onion in this frittata are great flavour companions to the smoky ham and cheese.

2 tablespoons (30 mL) butter

1 cup (250 mL) smoked ham, such as Black Forest, finely diced

1/2 cup (125 mL) finely diced, peeled apple

1/2 cup (125 mL) green onions (green part only), thinly sliced

1 cup (250 mL) finely shredded Applewood Smoked Cheddar cheese

8 large eggs, whisked in a small bowl with salt and freshly ground black pepper, to taste

1. Preheat broiler to low.

2. In a 10 inch (25 cm) cast iron or other oven-proof skillet, melt butter over medium heat. Add ham and apple and sauté for 3-4 minutes. Add onions and sauté for an additional 1-2 minutes.

3. Pour eggs over ham mixture in skillet. Stir to combine. Cook for 3-5 minutes, gently lifting the cooked edges with a spatula so the uncooked portion can flow to the bottom. Cook until eggs are nearly set but still moist on top. Remove from heat.

4. Sprinkle cheese on top of frittata.

5. Place the skillet under preheated broiler for 1-2 minutes to finish cooking eggs and to fully melt cheese.

6. Using 1 or 2 large spatulas, slip the frittata out onto a serving plate and cut into wedges to serve. Alternatively, the frittata can be served directly from the pan at the table.

Serves: 4-6

ON-THE-RUN BREAKFAST COOKIES

These will be a huge hit with everyone! Loaded with the goodness of grains, nuts, seeds, and dried fruits they are a terrific snack after school, for a hiking trip, or even a breakfast grain alternative.

To ease the preparation, assemble all the ingredients the night before you plan to make these cookies.

1 cup (250 mL) whole wheat flour

1/2 cup (125 mL) wheat germ

1 cup (250 mL) large flake oats

1 teaspoon (5 mL) baking powder

1/2 teaspoon (2.5 mL) salt

1 tablespoon (15 mL) ground cinnamon

1 teaspoon (5 mL) ground ginger

1/2 cup (125 mL) raisins

1 cup (250 mL) dried cranberries or cherries, coarsely chopped

1 cup (250 mL) coarsely chopped pecans

1/2 cup (125 mL) unsalted peanuts, coarsely chopped

1/2 cup (125 mL) chocolate chips

1/2 cup (125 mL) sunflower seeds

1/2 cup (125 mL) flax seeds

1/4 cup (125 mL) sesame seeds

1/4 cup (125 mL) poppy seeds

1 cup (250 mL) soft butter

1/2 cup (125 mL) peanut butter

1 1/4 cups (310 mL) lightly packed brown sugar

2 large eggs

1/4 cup (60 mL) 2% milk

1. Preheat oven to 350°F (180°C). Lightly grease two large baking sheets.

2. In a large mixing bowl, stir together flour, wheat germ, oats, baking powder, salt, cinnamon, and ginger. Add raisins, cranberries, nuts, chocolate chips, and seeds, and mix together with a spoon.

Continued…

ON-THE-RUN BREAKFAST COOKIES
continued...

Sunflower seeds are derived from the native North American sunflower. Here, they add a wonderful nutty taste and crunch to these popular cookies.

Sesame seeds come from a plant grown mostly in the hot climates of India, China, Mexico, and the Sudan. They are small seeds, ranging in colour from golden to brown to black. When crushed, they form the basis of the Middle Eastern specialty, tahini, or sesame paste. The extracted oil is also a common ingredient in Asian dishes, adding a nutty flavour.

3. In a separate, large mixing bowl, cream butter and peanut butter; add brown sugar and beat well. Add eggs one at a time and beat well after each addition. Add milk and stir to make a smooth mixture.

4. Add fruit/nut mixture to butter mixture and stir well with a wooden spoon until blended together.

5. Drop by 2 tablespoons (30 mL) 2 inches (5 cm) apart on lightly greased baking sheets. Flatten slightly with the back side of a fork.

6. Bake for 15-18 minutes until light brown and semi-firm to the touch.

7. Remove from oven; cool for 5 minutes and transfer to wire racks.

8. Store in airtight container.

Makes: 36-48 cookies

GREAT GRANOLA

The basis for many granola recipes is oats. The cleaned, toasted and hulled grain of the oat is often referred to as groats. They are further processed for a variety of uses.

Steel-cut oats are simply groats that are cut into two or four pieces for faster cooking.

Rolled oats or large flake oats are whole kernels that have been steamed to make them soft, and then pressed between rollers. The result is a thin product that quickly absorbs water when cooked.

Quick-cooking oats have been rolled thinner than rolled oats, to do what the name says – cook quicker.

Instant oats have been rolled the thinnest and cook the quickest.

4 cups (1 L) quick cooking oats

1/2 cup (125 mL) EACH:

- sliced almonds
- long-flake coconut
- shelled, unsalted sunflower seeds
- wheat germ
- wheat bran
- skim milk powder

1/2 cup (125 mL) honey

1/2 cup (125 mL) molasses

1 tablespoon (15 mL) ground cinnamon

1 teaspoon (5 mL) ground nutmeg

1. Preheat oven to 350°F (180°C). Lightly grease two large baking sheets or line with parchment paper.
2. In a large mixing bowl, combine oats, almonds, coconut, sunflower seeds, wheat germ, wheat bran, and skim milk powder. Stir to combine.
3. In a small saucepan, heat the honey, molasses, cinnamon, and nutmeg until warmed. Remove from heat and pour over oat/fruit/nut mixture and stir well to coat dry ingredients.
4. Spoon granola onto prepared baking sheets and spread evenly.
5. Bake for about 15 minutes or until mixture darkens slightly. Halfway through the baking, stir the mixture to ensure even cooking and prevent scorching.
6. Remove from oven and break into pieces. Cool before use or storage. Store in an airtight container.

Continued…

GREAT GRANOLA
continued...

Skim milk powder is a form of powdered milk from which almost all of the moisture has been removed. It has the beauty of a long shelf life, since most of the fat which could go rancid has been removed. Skim milk powder will keep for several months in cool, dry conditions. Today it is less often used a source of reconstituted fluid milk, but rather is used more in cooking and baking recipes such as in this versatile granola.

You can also add your own preferred taste ingredients to Great Granola such as:

- Dried fruit, including chopped apricots, cranberries, dates, cherries, blueberries, or raisins
- Sweet additions such as chocolate chips
- Other nuts such as toasted pecans or hazelnuts.

Makes: 6 cups

GRANOLA TRIFLE

6 cups (1.5 L) Great Granola (with added ingredients of your choice)

6 cups (1.5 L) vanilla yogurt

6 cups (1.5 L) cut up fruit, such as bananas, grapes, oranges, kiwi, and mangoes

1. In a large trifle bowl, layer 3 cups (750 mL) of granola; top with 3 cups (750 mL) of yogurt and 3 cups (750 mL) of fruit. Repeat.
2. Alternatively, layer granola, yogurt, and fruit into sundae glasses and serve for breakfast.

Serves: 10-12

WHOLE GRAIN BREAD WITH OATS, FLAX, AND MILLET

These dense and delicious loaves are great to make on the weekend and freeze for later use.

Millet is a tiny, round, yellow cereal grass that, in North America, is used mostly for bird seed! However, in many other parts of the world, it is a cereal staple. It has a mild nutty flavour that lends itself well to the flavour of this bread.

Flaxseed originated in Eurasia and has been used for over 7,000 years as a food. The small, reddish-brown seed is glossy in appearance and has a nutty flavour. In cooking, flaxseed can be added whole to bread and other products, or can be ground and added to pancakes or meatloaf. You get the best nutrition from the seed if it's ground. The whole seed is used in this bread, where it adds a wonderful 'crunch'.

1 1/2 cups (375 mL) 2% milk
1/2 cup (125 mL) brown sugar
2 teaspoons (10 mL) salt
1/2 cup (125 mL) large flake oats
1/2 cup (125 mL) whole flax seed
1/2 cup (125 mL) medium or fine cracked wheat
1/2 cup (125 mL) millet
1 1/2 cups (375 mL) water, warmed to 115°F (45°C)
2 teaspoons (10 mL) sugar
2 tablespoons (30 mL) active dry yeast
3 cups (750 mL) all-purpose flour
1 cup (25 mL) barley flour
2 cups (500 mL) whole wheat flour

1. In a medium sauce pot, heat milk until hot but not boiling. Remove from heat. Add brown sugar and salt and stir to dissolve. Add oats, flax, cracked wheat, and millet. Stir to combine and let stand at room temperature for one hour to soften grains.

2. In a separate large bowl, combine warm water, sugar, and yeast. Let stand until frothy, about 10 minutes. Add softened grains and mix. Add the flours and stir with a wooden spoon to combine. Add more all-purpose flour if necessary to make a stiff dough.

3. Remove to a lightly floured work surface and knead for 10-12 minutes. Place in a large, greased mixing bowl. Cover with plastic wrap and let rise in a warm spot until double in bulk, about 1 hour.

4. Punch dough down and let rise again in a warm spot for 1 hour.

Continued...

WHOLE GRAIN BREAD WITH OATS, FLAX, AND MILLET

continued...

Aside from its role in making beer, barley is a much underutilized grain. Whole grain barley flour is a great source of dietary fibre and B vitamins. If you want to use more barley flour, you can substitute it cup for cup of all-purpose flour when making muffins, quick breads, and cookies. When making yeast products, up to 1/4 of the flour can generally be replaced with barley flour.

Cracked wheat is the whole wheat berry crushed into either coarse, medium, or fine grains. Medium or fine cracked wheat works best in this recipe.

5. Form dough into two loaves. Place in lightly greased 9x5 inch (2 L) loaf pans. Cover with plastic wrap and let rise again for 45 minutes.

6. Remove plastic wrap and bake in a preheated 375°F (190°C) oven for 35 minutes or until loaf sounds hollow when tapped on the top.

7. Remove from baking pans and let cool on wire racks.

Makes: 2 loaves

YOGURT PANCAKES

My friend's husband made these for us one day for breakfast. What a delicious treat and even better when served by one of our husbands! Seven-grain cereal is often available in bulk in grocery stores.

3 large eggs, beaten

3/4 cup (175 mL) plain or vanilla yogurt

1 cup (250 mL) 2% milk

1/4 cup (60 mL) melted butter

1 1/2 cups (375 mL) all-purpose flour (or 1 cup [250 mL] all-purpose flour and 1/2 cup [125 mL] 7-grain cereal mix)

1 teaspoon (5 mL) baking soda

2 teaspoons (10 mL) baking powder

1 teaspoon (5 mL) salt

1 tablespoon (15 mL) sugar

1. In a small mixing bowl, combine eggs, yogurt, milk, and butter until smooth.

2. In another medium mixing bowl, stir together flour, baking soda, baking powder, salt, and sugar.

3. Add wet ingredients to dry and stir just to combine; a few lumps will remain. Let batter sit 5-10 minutes before cooking. Batter will begin to swell; just stir to remove the air before cooking.

4. Heat a grill or non-stick skillet to high. Lightly grease with cooking spray or butter. Pour 1/4 cup (60 mL) batter on to hot skillet (will spread to make about a 4 inch [10 cm] pancake). Cook until small bubbles form on surface, about 1 minute; flip and cook for 1 more minute until golden brown.

5. If needed, transfer to warm plate and keep warm in 200°F (95°C) oven while cooking remaining pancakes.

Makes: about 10, 4 inch (10 cm) pancakes

SOUP'S ON!

Nothing warms the soul better than soup, especially on a cold fall or winter day and especially if it's homemade! Be it hearty and full of vegetables or clear and simple, what makes a soup good is its body, texture, and of course, flavour.

Body is somewhat difficult to describe, but an Austrian chef instructor of mine did a pretty good job. When he tasted a soup with good body, he said his mouth came alive and he could feel the soup almost penetrate his cheeks. A soup with good body fills your mouth as opposed to just slipping down your throat.

Soup with good texture should reflect the type of soup that it is. For example, if the soup is supposed to be smooth and creamy, such as Cream of Many Mushrooms (page 42), then it should be velvety in texture and free of any starchy lumps. If the soup is a complex vegetable soup, such as Borscht (page 33), then the broth should be clear and all the vegetable ingredients should be identifiable, not one large, soft mass.

As for flavour, the soup should be full flavoured, and the flavours from each of the ingredients should be easy to identify. The best test of flavour, of course, is how quickly it disappears from the table!

Clear soups include broth-based soups made from meat, poultry, game, fish, or vegetable stocks. Ideally, stock should be used to make a truly superior soup. However, this is not often practical in a home setting, and commercially prepared broths are a suitable substitute. You can also sometimes purchase prepared stocks from restaurants or farmers' markets, but they tend to be quite expensive. Powdered soup bases are also available in the grocery stores, but in my opinion, should only be used as a last choice as they are often poor in flavour and very high in salt.

Thickened soups include cream soups and pureed soups. Classical cream soups are prepared by first cooking vegetables such as mushrooms, broccoli, or cauliflower in a liquid (stock or broth). The mixture is then thickened with starch, pureed, and finally cream is added to give richness and flavour. People sometimes shy away from cream soups as they are often very high in fat and calories. If you want to reduce the fat from cream in a soup, you can use half cream and half milk, or evaporated skim or 2% milk. Pureed soups such as pea or carrot are made by first simmering the vegetable in a liquid and then pureeing the soup to achieve the desired consistency. Starch is rarely added to pureed soups.

Chowders are hearty soups with larger pieces of vegetables, potatoes, and sometimes meat or fish. The most common chowders are clam and seafood, but other combinations such as Spicy Vegetable Chowder with Nut Butter (page 50) and Veggie Cheddar Chowder (page 48) are also very tasty!

AVGOLEMONO

This is a delightful and light soup with Greek origin. It's simple to make, but does require some careful technique so as not to curdle the eggs. The key to success lies in step 3, where you carefully and slowly add some hot broth to the egg mixture. Care has to be taken here – if you add the hot broth too much at a time or too quickly, the heat will shock the eggs and they will curdle, or cook, and you will end up with scrambled egg soup. I know this – I've done it! If this happens, the soup will not be spoiled and it's still safe to eat, but it won't look very appealing. So take care and enjoy this luscious, springtime soup.

8 cups (2 L) chicken stock or broth

3/4 cup (175 mL) long grain white rice

4 large eggs

1 teaspoon (5 mL) all-purpose flour

1/2 cup (125 mL) fresh lemon juice

Salt and white pepper to taste

Chopped parsley for garnish

1. Bring chicken stock or broth to boil. Add raw rice, reduce heat to a simmer, and cook for about 20 minutes until rice is tender.

2. Meanwhile, in a medium bowl, beat eggs and flour with a whisk, until light yellow in colour, about 1 minute. Slowly add lemon juice, stirring to combine.

3. From the cooked broth/rice mixture, ladle about 2 cups (500 mL) of soup into a medium bowl. Very slowly, begin to add hot broth to the egg mixture, starting with 1/4 cup (60 mL) and stirring constantly after each addition. When all of the broth has been added, return the egg/broth mixture to the heated broth/rice mixture. Heat gently. Do not boil as the mixture may curdle.

4. Garnish with chopped parsley. Serve with Pink Grapefruit and Avocado Salad with Poppy Seed Dressing (page 151) and fresh whole grain buns for a simple tasty meal.

Serves: 6-8

BORSCHT

Make this flavourful soup of Russian and Polish descent when fresh beets are available. Your hands will get 'beet stained' from grating the beets – use plastic gloves if you want to avoid red hands. Borscht (or sometimes, Borsch) can be served hot or cold, but always with a dollop of sour cream. With the added meat, it makes a hearty meal.

A sachet is a classical way to add flavour to a soup made simply by taking a (6 inch [15 cm] square) piece of cheesecloth, laying the ingredients on it, and then bringing all the sides together, and tying it with string. The sachet is added to the soup and later removed by the string when the soup has finished cooking. Be careful with the cloves. When I first made this soup in cooking school, I added 12, not 2, cloves to my sachet – to promptly produce 'clove soup' and a horrible face on my chef instructor!

2 tablespoons (30 mL) vegetable oil

1 cup (250 mL) finely diced onions

3/4 cup (175 mL) finely sliced leeks, white part only

1 cup (250 mL) finely shredded white cabbage

1/2 cup (125 mL) finely diced carrots

1/2 cup (125 mL) finely diced celery

8 cups (2 L) beef stock or broth, simmering

1 sachet made of: 6 parsley stems
2 bay leaves
10 whole black peppercorns
2 whole cloves

1 pound (500 g) fresh beets, peeled and grated

1/4 cup (60 mL) white vinegar

3/4 pound (375 g) cooked roast beef, cut into thin strips (optional)

1 tablespoon (15 mL) finely chopped fresh dill

Salt and freshly ground black pepper, to taste

Sour cream, for garnish

1. In a large sauce pot, heat oil on medium heat. Add onions, leeks, cabbage, carrots, and celery and cook until vegetables are soft, about 10 minutes.

2. Add simmering stock and sachet. Simmer for 1 1/2 hours. Remove sachet.

3. Add beets, vinegar, beef, and fresh dill. Simmer for 20 minutes. Taste and adjust seasoning with salt and pepper.

4. Ladle soup into bowls and garnish with a dollop of sour cream.

Serve with a wedge of sourdough or rye bread.

Serves: 6-8

SPICED CARROT SOUP

It doesn't get much simpler than this to make a light and nutritious soup. The mild flavour of carrots is brought to life with fresh ginger and ground nutmeg. For a taste variation, you can use 1/2 cup (125 mL) of orange juice to replace some of the chicken broth. This soup is low in calories and packed with beta-carotene.

This soup is also great if made the day before serving as the flavours intensify. If the soup becomes too thick, add more stock or broth.

1 tablespoon (15 mL) vegetable oil

1/2 cup (125 mL) chopped celery

1/4 cup (60 mL) coarsely chopped onion

2 cups (500 mL) carrots, sliced about 1/2 inch (1 cm) thick

2 1/2 cups (625 mL) chicken or vegetable stock or broth

1 tablespoon (15 mL) finely grated fresh ginger root

1/2 teaspoon (2.5 mL) ground nutmeg

Freshly ground white pepper, to taste

Salt, to taste

Sour cream, for garnish

Finely snipped chives, for garnish

1. Heat oil in a medium saucepan over medium heat. Add celery and onion and cook only until vegetables become soft and translucent, about 3 minutes-do not allow any browning to take place or you'll have little brown bits in your smooth soup. Add carrots and stock or broth. Bring to boil over medium high heat. Reduce heat to low and simmer, covered for 30 minutes. Remove from heat and allow to cool for about 20 minutes.

2. Transfer soup to a food processor and puree until smooth.

3. Return soup to a clean pot and heat until hot. Add ginger root and nutmeg, stir to combine, and heat over medium heat an additional 10 minutes. Season with salt and pepper to taste.

4. Ladle into bowls and garnish each bowl with a dollop of sour cream and snipped chives before serving.

Serve with Spinach Salad with Fresh Nectarines, Raspberries, and Candied Almonds (page 152).

Serves: 4-6

HEARTY LENTIL SOUP

This soup was traditionally served in our home on New Year's Eve at midnight to symbolize good luck for the upcoming year.

1/2 pound (250 g) bacon, pepper edged if possible, chopped into 1/2 inch (1 cm) dice

1 cup (250 mL) coarsely chopped cooked Kielbasa sausage

1 cup (250 mL) finely diced onions

1/2 cup (125 mL) finely diced carrots

4 garlic cloves, finely minced

8 cups (2 L) chicken broth or stock

19-ounce (540 mL) can diced tomatoes, drained

1 pound (500 g) green lentils, washed well and picked over to remove any debris

1 cup (250 mL) coarsely chopped flat-leaf parsley

2 teaspoons (10 mL) dried oregano

1 1/2 (7.5 mL) teaspoons salt

1 teaspoon (5 mL) freshly ground black pepper

1. Heat a large sauce pot or Dutch oven to medium high and add bacon to cook. Stir often to be sure it doesn't become crisp. Cook for about 3 minutes to render some of the fat and then add Kielbasa, onions, carrots, and garlic. Cook and stir for about 5-8 minutes until vegetables are tender and translucent but not browned.

2. Add chicken broth or stock, tomatoes, lentils, parsley, oregano, and 1 teaspoon (5 mL) each salt and pepper. Stir well and bring to a boil. Reduce to a simmer and cook until lentils are soft, about 30-40 minutes.

3. Taste and adjust seasoning with additional salt and pepper.

Serves: 6-8

ITALIAN WEDDING SOUP

It's called Italian Wedding soup because it's traditionally served at Italian weddings! When I worked in a large cafeteria, the commercial form of this soup was the favourite of patrons. Homemade, it's absolutely delicious! Don't be distressed if, when you add the meatballs to the broth, 'bits and pieces' shred into the broth – it's simply the result of adding raw meatballs to hot liquid. If you don't like this look, you can cook the meatballs separately in boiling water, strain them, and add to the cooked soup.

I know it may seem like a lot of work to get 3 different kinds of meat for the meatballs, but it really does make the best meatballs, in my opinion. However, if you prefer, you can use entirely ground beef.

Meatballs:

1/2 cup (125 mL) finely minced onion

1/4 pound (125 g) EACH finely ground beef, veal, and pork

1 large egg

1/4 cup (60 mL) fine, dry breadcrumbs

1/4 cup (60 mL) finely grated Parmesan cheese

1/2 teaspoon (2.5 mL) EACH salt and freshly grated black pepper

1 teaspoon (5 mL) dried basil

Soup:

8 cups (2 L) chicken stock or broth

2, 10-ounce packages (284 g) frozen spinach, defrosted, well-drained, and coarsely chopped

2/3 cup (150 mL) dry orzo pasta

1/2 cup (125 mL) finely diced carrots

Salt and freshly ground black pepper, to taste

1/2 cup (125 mL) Parmesan cheese, for garnish

Chopped fresh parsley, for garnish

For meatballs:

1. In a large mixing bowl, combine all ingredients for meatballs and mix well.

2. Make tiny meatballs (about 1/2 inch [1 cm] diameter) and place on a parchment-lined baking sheet; refrigerate until ready to use.

Continued...

Italian Wedding Soup
page 36

Grape Tomato Salad with Olives, Cucumbers, and Fennel

page 150

ITALIAN WEDDING SOUP
continued...

For soup:

1. Pour chicken stock or broth into a large sauce pot. Bring to a boil, then reduce heat to simmer.

2. Meanwhile, in a separate pot, bring 8 cups (2 L) salted water to a boil and cook orzo pasta until al dente. Drain and set aside.

3. Add the refrigerated meatballs to the simmering broth. Cook until meatballs are cooked through, about 8-10 minutes. Add drained spinach, cooked orzo, and carrots, and stir gently to combine. Simmer for additional 10 minutes.

4. Ladle soup into bowls and garnish with Parmesan cheese and chopped parsley.

Serve with crusty Italian bread and an assortment of Italian meats and cheeses.

Serves: 6-8

WHITE MINESTRONE SOUP

Minestrone refers to a 'big soup' of Italian origin that usually contains pasta and beans. It is generally used as a meal as it's quite hearty. Traditionally, it's made with a tomato base, but here the soup uses only white vegetables and beans. The cannellini beans used in this soup are a large, kidney-shaped, white Italian bean. The flavours get better after a day or two, so make it on the weekend to use for a weekday dinner.

2-3 tablespoons (30-45 mL) olive oil

1/4 pound (125 g) salt pork, finely chopped

1 bunch (4-5 cups [1-1.25 L]) fresh baby spinach, washed, stems removed, and coarsely chopped

1 cup (250 mL) finely chopped celery

1 large leek, white part only, finely sliced

1 bunch green onions (white and green parts), chopped

3 cups (750 mL) shredded white cabbage

1/4 cup (60 mL) freshly chopped parsley

19-ounce can (540 mL) cannellini beans, drained

8 cups (2 L) chicken broth or stock

1 cup (250 mL) dry orzo pasta

Salt and freshly ground pepper, to taste

Freshly grated Parmesan cheese, for garnish

1. In a large stock pot, heat oil and add salt pork. Cook over medium heat until much of the fat from the salt pork has been rendered.

2. Add spinach, celery, leeks, green onions, cabbage, and parsley and sauté for 5-7 minutes or until vegetables begin to wilt.

3. Add beans and broth; bring to a boil and then simmer for 30 minutes.

4. Meanwhile, in another medium sauce pot, cook orzo in boiling salted water until al dente. Drain and add to soup after the soup has simmered.

5. Season to taste with salt and pepper.

6. Garnish with freshly grated Parmesan cheese. Serve with fresh mozzarella and tomato salad and some peasant Italian bread.

Serves: 6-8

CLOVE-SCENTED TOMATO SOUP

There are so many canned tomato products to choose from, so here's a simple explanation.

Canned tomatoes come in various forms including whole, peeled, diced, and crushed. Very little has been done to these products except for the way they are cut.

Tomato puree is cooked and drained tomatoes resulting in a thick and rich product.

Tomato sauce, sometimes flavoured with herbs and spices, is thinned down tomato puree.

Tomato paste is the most concentrated form of canned tomatoes and is made by cooking tomatoes for several hours and then straining to produce a very rich and concentrated tomato product.

Be sure to pick the right type of canned tomato for the recipe you are making.

2 tablespoons (30 mL) butter

1/2 cup (125 mL) finely diced onions

1/4 teaspoon (1.25 mL) ground cloves

2 tablespoons (30 mL) all-purpose flour

2 cups (50 mL) chicken stock or broth

3/4 cup (175 mL) tomato juice

1 1/4 cups (310 mL) canned tomato puree

2 cups (500 mL) 2% milk, warmed, but not boiling

1 bay leaf

1 teaspoon (5 mL) salt

1/2 teaspoon (2.5 mL) black pepper

1 teaspoon (5 mL) sugar or more, to taste

1. In a large sauce pot, melt butter on medium heat and sauté onions for 2 minutes. Add cloves and flour and stir to combine. Cook and stir constantly for 1-2 minutes.

2. Add broth, 1 cup (250 mL) at a time, stirring well after each addition to make sure flour dissolves. Add tomato juice and tomato puree. Bring to a boil and then reduce to a simmer for 5-7 minutes.

3. Add warm milk and bay leaf and then simmer for an additional 30 minutes, being careful not to boil or the soup may curdle. Remove bay leaf and season with sugar, salt, and pepper. (The soup may require more sugar if the tomatoes are very acidic.)

Serve with rye croutons. To make croutons, slice rye bread slices into 3/4 inch (1.5 cm) cubes. Place on a baking sheet and toast in a preheated 375°F (190°C) oven until lightly toasted, about 10 minutes.

Serves: 4-6

CREAM OF MANY MUSHROOMS SOUP

Mushrooms have such a wonderful 'earthy' flavour to them. Using a variety of mushrooms adds interest and a wonderful melding of flavour to this soup. You can use any variety you like, or just use white mushrooms. You can get the full creaminess of a cream soup without all the fat, by using 2% milk for part of the stock or broth and then adding a small amount of cereal cream at the end to 'finish' the soup. This technique reduces the fat significantly and yields a creamy, but less heavy, soup.

1/2 pound (250 g) EACH white, brown, shiitake, and portobello mushrooms

1/4 cup (60 mL) butter

1/2 cup (125 mL) butter

1 cup (250 mL) finely diced onions

1/2 cup (125 mL) all-purpose flour

6 cups (1.5 L) chicken stock or broth

2 cups (500 mL) 2% milk

1 sachet filled with 10 peppercorns, 1 bay leaf, 4 parsley stems to make a sachet, see page 33)

4 stems fresh thyme (do not substitute dried thyme leaves or ground thyme)

Salt and freshly ground black pepper, to taste

1/2 cup (125 mL) cereal cream (10% MF)

1/2 cup (125 mL) chopped parsley, for garnish

1. Slice all mushrooms into 1/4 inch (.5 cm) slices; be sure to remove and discard thick stems from shiitake mushrooms, remove stem and veins from portobello mushrooms.

2. In a large non-stick skillet, melt 1/4 cup (60 mL) butter, add mushrooms, and cook until they are softened but not browned, about 5-8 minutes. Remove from heat and set aside to cool.

3. In a large sauce pot, melt 1/2 cup (125 mL) butter and cook onions until translucent but not brown. Add flour and stir to make a thick paste-cook slightly, about 1-2 minutes, stirring constantly. Add broth, 1 cup (250 mL) at a time, stirring well to blend with flour mixture after each addition. Add milk, sachet, thyme and cooked mushrooms. Bring to a low boil.

Continued...

NUTMEG-SCENTED CREAMY CAULIFLOWER SOUP

continued...

1/4 cup (60 mL) cereal cream (optional)

1 tablespoon (15 mL) chopped cilantro

2 cups (500 mL) small cauliflower florets, blanched for 5 minutes in boiling water and refreshed in cold water

1. In large sauce pot, melt butter. Add diced onions, carrots, celery, cauliflower, and garlic, and sauté vegetables for 3-4 minutes until they begin to soften.

2. Add flour to combine; stir constantly and cook for 1-2 minutes.

3. Add thyme and nutmeg, stir and cook for 1-2 minutes to release flavours.

4. Add simmering vegetable stock, 1 cup (250 mL) at a time, blending well after each addition. Add bay leaf. Bring to a boil, then reduce heat and simmer for 30 minutes. Remove from heat and let cool for about 20 minutes. Remove bay leaf and thyme sprigs.

5. Transfer soup to a food processor and purée in small batches until smooth. Return soup to sauce pot. Season to taste with additional salt and white pepper. Stir in cream (if using) and heat thoroughly, but do not boil. Top with the blanched cauliflower florets and chopped cilantro.

Serve with a fresh green salad with a tart dressing and whole grain buns.

Serves: 6-8

CURRIED CREAM OF BROCCOLI SOUP

You can vary the fat content of cream soups considerably by your choice of cream or milk. The higher the 'BF' (butterfat) or 'MF' (milk fat) content of the milk or cream, the more fat it contains. The approximate fat content of creams and milks in descending order is:

Whipping cream (about 35% MF)

Coffee or table cream (about 15-18% MF)

Cereal cream or 'half and half' (about 10% MF)

Whole milk (about 3.25% MF)

2% milk (about 2% MF)

Skim milk (less than .5% MF)

You can also substitute other frozen vegetables such as spinach or asparagus for the broccoli in this soup.

2 cups (500 mL) chicken or vegetable stock or broth
2, 10-ounce (284 g) packages frozen, chopped broccoli
1/2 cup (125 mL) chopped onion
2 tablespoons (30 mL) butter
2 tablespoons (30 mL) all-purpose flour
1 teaspoon (5 mL) hot curry powder
1/2 teaspoon (2.5 mL) salt
1/2 cup cereal (125 mL) cream (10% MF)
1 1/2 cups (375 mL) 2 % milk
Salt and freshly ground white pepper

1. In a medium size pot, bring chicken or vegetable stock or broth to a simmer and add frozen broccoli and onion. Simmer for 10 minutes until tender. Remove from heat and let cool for about 20 minutes. (I find it easier and safer to purée hot mixtures when they've cooled slightly).

2. Transfer mixture to food processor and purée broccoli mixture until smooth. Set aside.

3. In a large saucepot, melt butter and add flour, curry powder and salt. Cook, stirring constantly for 1-2 minutes. Add warm puréed broccoli mixture to flour mixture, 1 cup (250 mL) at a time, stirring well after each addition.

4. Add cream and milk. Heat, but do not boil.

5. Adjust seasoning with salt and pepper and serve.

6. Optional: you can 1 cup (250 mL) grated aged Cheddar cheese to the soup at the end. Stir well to melt cheese.

Serves: 4-6

SAVOURY PUMPKIN SOUP

This is a wonderful soup for a fall day. It's rich and creamy and filled with great nutrition, including beta carotene from the red pepper and pumpkin, and calcium from the milk.

2 tablespoons (30 mL) butter

1 cup (250 mL) finely chopped red bell pepper

1 cup (25 mL) finely chopped onion

2 tablespoons (30 mL) all-purpose flour

1 teaspoon (5 mL) salt

3 cups (750 mL) chicken or vegetable stock or broth

2 cups (500 mL) pumpkin purée

2 cups (500 mL) 2% milk

2 sprigs fresh thyme

1/2 teaspoon (2.5 mL) ground nutmeg

1 tablespoon (15 mL) finely snipped chives

Salt and freshly ground black pepper

1. In a large sauce pot, on medium heat, melt butter. Sauté pepper and onions until soft but not browned.

2. Blend in flour and salt. Cook for 3-4 minutes. Stir constantly so as not to scorch.

3. Add chicken or vegetable stock or broth, pumpkin purée, milk, thyme and nutmeg, Bring to a boil, then reduce to a simmer for 10-15 minutes. If the soup is too thick, add more stock or broth.

4. Remove thyme sprigs. Adjust seasoning with salt and freshly ground pepper. Garnish with chives.

Serve with slices of Whole Grain Bread with Oats, Flax, and Millet (page 28) and a fresh green salad and you've got a lovely lunch or light supper.

Serves: 6-8

VEGGIE CHEDDAR CHOWDER

This is a perfect soup to make on a winter's day when you have some time to chop vegetables. It's loaded with flavour and great nutrition from vegetables, milk, and cheese. Add a fresh green salad and whole grain buns for a simple meal.

2 tablespoons (30 mL) vegetable oil

1/2 cup (125 mL) finely diced onions

1/2 cup (125 mL) finely diced carrots

1/2 cup (125 mL) finely diced celery

3/4 cup (175 mL) finely diced red bell pepper

2 jalapeno peppers, seeded, de-veined and finely diced

4 garlic cloves, finely minced

1 tablespoon (15 mL) ground cumin

1 teaspoon (5 mL) ground oregano

1/2 teaspoon (2.5 mL) dried thyme leaves (do not use ground thyme)

3 tablespoons (45 mL) all-purpose flour

6 cups (1.5 L) warm vegetable or chicken stock or broth

1 cup (250 mL) frozen corn, defrosted

2 cups (500 mL) 2% milk, warmed

1/2 cup (125 mL) cereal cream (10% MF)

1 tablespoon (15 mL) fresh chopped cilantro

1 1/2 cups (375 mL) grated aged Cheddar or Gruyere cheese

Salt and freshly ground black pepper

1. In a large sauce pot, heat oil and sauté onions, carrots, celery, and peppers until soft. Add garlic and sauté one additional minute.

2. Add cumin, oregano, thyme, and flour. Stir and cook constantly for 1-2 minutes until flavours are released and flour is slightly cooked.

Continued...

VEGGIE CHEDDAR CHOWDER
continued...

3. Pour in stock, 1 cup (250 mL) at a time, stirring well after each addition. Bring to a boil and then simmer for 30 minutes. Add corn, warmed milk, cream, and cilantro. Stir to combine and heat thoroughly, but do not boil.

4. Stir in grated cheese until melted.

5. Adjust seasoning with salt and freshly ground pepper.

Serves: 8-10

SPICY VEGETABLE CHOWDER WITH NUT BUTTER

This hearty chowder is a great infusion of vegetable flavours. It can be made truly vegetarian if you use vegetable stock (page 44). A food processor simplifies the chopping. You can use either peanut butter or almond butter in this chowder. The peanut butter will give a very smooth soup, whereas the almond butter will leave some fine texture from the ground almonds. Both taste great! If this chowder is not eaten the day it's made, it will become quite thick. To reheat, you may need to thin it down with added water or broth.

1 teaspoon (5 mL) sesame oil

2 teaspoons (10 mL) vegetable oil

3/4 cup (175 mL) coarsely chopped onion

1/3 cup (75 mL) finely chopped red pepper

3 garlic cloves, finely minced

1/2 cup (125 mL) finely chopped celery

1/2 cup (125 mL) finely chopped cauliflower

1/2 cup (125 mL) finely chopped, peeled parsnips

2/3 cup (150 mL) finely chopped carrots

2 cups (500 mL) peeled sweet potatoes, cut into 1/2 inch (1 cm) dice

4 cups (1 L) vegetable broth or chicken stock or broth

1/4 teaspoon (1.25 mL) ground cayenne pepper

1/2 teaspoon (2.5 mL) salt

1 teaspoon (5 mL) freshly ground black pepper

Pinch ground nutmeg

1/2 cup (125 mL) smooth peanut butter OR almond butter

1/2 cup (125 mL) finely chopped, unsalted peanuts OR toasted almonds

1. Heat oils in sauce pot. Add onion and red pepper and sauté until tender. Add garlic and sauté an additional one minute. Add celery, cauliflower, parsnips, carrots, sweet potatoes, and stock or broth. Bring to a boil. Reduce heat and simmer about 30 minutes.

2. Add cayenne pepper, salt, black pepper, nutmeg, and peanut butter (or almond butter) and stir until smooth.

3. Transfer mixture to food processor and process until smooth. Adjust seasoning with salt and pepper as needed. Serve and garnish with chopped peanuts (or almonds).

Serves: 4-6

FOR STARTERS...

Excite your palate! That's the job of a starter or appetizer. Starters are often spicy and pungent as they get your appetite ready for what's still to come. Some of the starters that follow can be easily used on an appetizer buffet table while some are more suited to a first course for a meal. Regardless of their use, they should all whet your whistle!

Whenever I serve a starter as a first course, I like to keep it flavourful, but not teeming with calories. If it's too 'heavy', your guests will simply be too full to fully enjoy The Main Event. To start your next dinner off just right try the Cajun Baked Shrimp, Grilled Mediterranean Vegetable Strata with Sun-dried Tomato Vinaigrette, or Steamed Prawn and Scallop Ravioli with Carrot and Ginger Broth.

If you're hosting a cocktail party and want to serve an appetizer buffet, here are a couple 'rules of thumb' to help you out:

How much should I make?

- If you're serving only an appetizer buffet, plan on 10-12 appetizer portions per person; if the buffet is followed by a meal, serve less and plan on 4-6 appetizer portions per person.

What should I make?

- An ideal appetizer buffet consists of hot and cold appetizers. I find it best to have the cold appetizers scattered throughout the room when people arrive. This avoids congestion at a buffet table and gets people mingling. A nice selection of cold appetizers includes a tray of cheese, fruit and crackers, dips and spreads and other 'finger' foods. Then, bring out hot appetizers as the night progresses; this way your guests get to try new appetizers occasionally, they will be piping hot, and you get to mingle with your guests as you serve them.

How do I manage the work?

- Plan ahead. Make sure you have enough refrigerator space for ingredients and finished products, enough oven space to cook hot items, enough plates (1-2 per person) and napkins (4-5 per person) and enough ice.
- Make as many items ahead as possible and be sure you keep them at a safe food temperature.
- Be sure you have accessible garbage bins for people to discard refuse.
- Make sure the event remains fun for you and your guest and always remember to keep Flavour First!

BRIE WITH CRANAPPLE CHUTNEY AND TOASTED PECANS

Nothing quite says fall like the flavours of apples, cranberries, and the sweet spices of cinnamon and allspice. This time-saving chutney cooks in the microwave oven and makes a delightful accompaniment atop melted Brie.

Allspice is not a combination of 'all spices', although its flavour mimics a combination of cinnamon, nutmeg, and cloves. Allspice is native to the West Indies, South America, and Jamaica, where it is a berry of the evergreen pimiento tree. It can be purchased as whole berries, which are often added to pickling spices or marinades for a sweet flavour, but more often is purchased ground and traditionally used in pumpkin pie.

6 inch (15 cm) round Brie (or Camembert)

Cranapple Chutney

For Cranapple Chutney:

2 large tart cooking apples (such as Granny Smith), peeled, cored, and finely diced

1/2 cup (125 mL) dried cranberries

1/2 cup (125 mL) lightly packed brown sugar

1/3 cup (75 mL) apple cider vinegar

1/3 cup (75 mL) finely diced red onion

1 teaspoon (5 mL) finely grated orange zest

1/4 teaspoon (1.25 mL) salt

1 teaspoon (5 mL) finely grated fresh ginger

1/4 teaspoon (1.25 mL) ground cinnamon

1/4 teaspoon (1.25 mL) ground allspice

1/2 cup (125 mL) chopped, toasted pecans

1. Combine all ingredients, except nuts, in a medium microwave-safe bowl. Cook on high, covered for about 10 minutes, stirring once.

2. Uncover and cook another 5 minutes on high. The mixture should be thick and slightly sticky.

Assembly:

1. Preheat oven to 350°F (180°C). Place cheese on ovenproof baking dish. Spoon 1-1 1/2 cups (250-375 mL) chutney on top. Save the rest of the chutney to use as an accompaniment to another meal or serve on the side.

2. Bake 10-15 minutes or until cheese is softened and begins to ooze. Remove from oven and top with pecans.

Continued...

BRIE WITH CRANAPPLE CHUTNEY AND TOASTED PECANS
continued...

3. Return to oven to bake for an additional 5 minutes.
4. Remove from oven and let rest for 10-15 minutes before serving so that cheese firms slightly.
5. Serve with French baguette slices and assorted crackers.

Makes: 1 large round of cheese

CAJUN BAKED SHRIMP

The word Cajun is derived from 'Acadians'. The Cajuns of the southern United States are descendents of the French Acadians that were forced from Nova Scotia in the late 1700s by the British, eventually settling in the Southern US. Although many people use the terms interchangeably and both prevail in the Southern US, Cajun and Creole are distinct cuisines. Cajun cuisine is a combination of French and Southern cuisine that relies heavily on the use of spices. Creole cuisine is often tomato-based and uses plenty of butter and cream.

1/2 cup (125 mL) extra virgin olive oil

2 tablespoons (30 mL) commercially prepared Cajun seasoning

2 tablespoons (30 mL) fresh lemon juice

2 tablespoons (30 mL) chopped fresh parsley

1 tablespoon (15 mL) honey

1 tablespoon (15 mL) soy sauce

1 pound (500 g) peeled and de-veined large shrimp, about 16-20 per pound (500 g)

1. In a glass or ceramic mixing bowl, combine first 6 ingredients and blend well.

2. Add shrimp and stir to coat. Cover and marinate in the refrigerator for 12-18 hours.

3. Remove shrimp from marinade and place on baking sheet; discard marinade.

4. Bake in preheated 425°F (215°C) oven for about 10 minutes or until shrimp are fully pink, depending on the size of the shrimp.

5. Remove to a serving dish and serve with picks as an appetizer, or serve on a bed of hot steamed rice as a first course.

Serves: 4-6

Creole Shrimp Cocktail
page 60

Roasted Eggplant and Red Pepper Antipasto with Fresh Herbs
page 67

CAMEMBERT WITH SHERRIED MUSHROOMS IN PUFF PASTRY

Sherry is a fortified wine traditionally made in Southern Spain, but, as with many wines and liquors, other countries are now producing it.

A medium priced, medium dry sherry works well in this recipe. And, you can have a sip while you're making it!

2 tablespoons (30 mL) butter

2 tablespoons (30 mL) finely minced shallots

2 cups (500 mL) sliced fresh white mushrooms

2 tablespoons (30 mL) sherry

1 teaspoon (5 mL) Worcestershire sauce

1/2 teaspoon (2.5 mL) dried tarragon

1 teaspoon (5 mL) fresh thyme leaves

1/4 teaspoon (1.25 mL) freshly ground black pepper

2 tablespoons (30 mL) fine dry breadcrumbs

1/2 of 14 oz (397 g) box of frozen puff pastry, defrosted

3- or 4 inch (7.5-10 cm) round of Camembert or Brie

1 egg yolk mixed with 1 teaspoon (5 mL) water, for brushing

1. In a large skillet, sauté shallots and mushrooms in butter for 3-4 minutes until golden. Add sherry, Worcestershire sauce, tarragon, thyme, and pepper. Stir and cook for one minute. Add breadcrumbs to soak up any remaining moisture and cook for 1 more minute. Remove from heat and set aside.

2. Preheat oven to 400°F (200°C). Roll out puff pastry to 9 or 10 inches (23-25 cm) square. Place mushroom mixture in centre. Top with cheese. Pull up each corner of the pastry and pinch together ensuring the cheese is fully encased. Make 2 or 3 slits with a knife to allow steam to escape during cooking. Brush with egg yolk mixture. Place in lightly greased, oven proof baking dish.

3. Bake for 20-25 minutes until golden. Remove from oven and let rest 20-30 minutes before serving. Serve with your favourite crackers or baguette slices. This is lovely served alongside a plate of freshly sliced pears and red and green grapes.

Serves: 6-8

CLASSIC BRUSCHETTA WITH TOMATOES AND BASIL

Contrary to the popular belief that bruschetta is the tomato and basil topping traditionally placed on bread rounds, bruschetta actually is the bread! This crisp bread, which can be topped with countless savoury toppings, is made by rubbing slices of toasted baguette or ciabatta bread with garlic and then drizzling it with high quality, flavourful olive oil. Bruschetta is often served on its own at Italian tables, but we've come to expect it topped. Here's one of my simple favourites.

For the best flavour, use the very freshest tomatoes you can find.

8 ripe plum tomatoes, coarsely chopped

3/4 cup (175 mL) coarsely chopped fresh basil

1 tablespoon (15 mL) finely minced fresh garlic

1 tablespoon (15 mL) dried oregano

1 tablespoon (15 mL) balsamic vinegar

2-3 tablespoons (30-45 mL) extra virgin olive oil

Salt and freshly ground black pepper

10-12 shaved slices of Parmesan cheese

Bruschetta:

1 loaf ciabatta bread, cut into 10-12 slices

4 fresh garlic cloves, split in half

About 1 tablespoon (15 mL) olive oil

1. In a large mixing bowl, place tomatoes, basil, 1 tablespoon (15 mL) fresh garlic, oregano, balsamic vinegar, and 1 tablespoon (15 mL) olive oil. Stir well to combine. Season with salt and pepper.

For bruschetta:

Preheat oven to 400°F (200°C). Place bread slices on a baking sheet and toast each side lightly. Remove from the oven. Rub each piece of bread with half a clove of fresh garlic and brush lightly with olive oil.

To serve:

Place about 2 tablespoons (30 mL) tomato mixture on bruschetta. Top with Parmesan cheese and serve.

Makes: 10-12 appetizer servings

DILLED SALMON SPREAD

Here's a quick lesson in the variations of smoked salmon. Fresh salmon is smoked using either hot or cold methods. In the hot method, the fish is smoked for 6-12 hours at a temperature of 120-180°F (49-60°C). In a cold smoke, lower temperatures are used and the fish can smoke anywhere from 1 day to 3 weeks. To make gravlax, often referred to simply as 'lox', the raw salmon is brine cured (added salt and sugar) and cold smoked, then sliced paper-thin.

For this recipe, spare your wallet and use yet another type of smoked salmon found in the meat/fish section of most supermarkets. It is often called Barbecued Salmon Tips or Smoked Salmon Tips. It's the whole fish (not paper thin slices) and will easily 'flake' when mixed.

1/2 pound (225 g) smoked peppered salmon tips

1/2 cup (125 mL) finely diced English cucumber

1/4 cup (60 mL) finely diced red onion

1 tablespoon (15 mL) finely snipped fresh dill

1/2 cup (125 mL) mayonnaise, regular or fat-reduced

2 tablespoons (30 mL) Dijon mustard

1. In a small mixing bowl, use a fork to break up salmon and then add remaining ingredients. Stir until well mixed. Do not over mix.

2. Serve with your favourite cracker, mini pita breads, toasted rye bread points, savoury cream puffs, or crostini.

Makes: 1 1/2 cups (375 mL)

CREOLE SHRIMP COCKTAIL

Shrimp cocktail gets its name from being served in a 'cocktail' glass – one with a stem. The sauce for this version goes well beyond the typical ketchup and horseradish sauce! Creole mustard is unique among the prepared mustards and is made from marinated mustard seeds with added horseradish and other seasonings. If you can't find Creole mustard, substitute a grainy brown mustard. You can turn the heat up on this sauce by adding more hot pepper sauce if you like.

2 celery ribs, cut into thirds

4 green onions (green part only), cut into thirds

1 small yellow onion, cut into quarters

3/4 cup (175 mL) lightly packed fresh parsley leaves

1/2 cup (125 mL) red wine vinegar

1/2 cup (125 mL) ketchup

1/2 cup (125 mL) tomato paste

1/2 cup (125 mL) Creole mustard

2 tablespoons (30 mL) prepared horseradish

2 teaspoons (10 mL) Worcestershire sauce

1/2 teaspoon (2.5 mL) EACH salt and freshly ground black pepper and hot pepper sauce such as Tabasco®

1/2 cup (125 mL) vegetable oil

2 pounds (1 kg) cooked, chilled fresh large shrimp, peeled and de-veined (about 16-20 per pound [500 g])

Bibb lettuce leaves

Chopped fresh parsley for garnish

Creole Sauce:

1. In a food processor, pulse celery, green onions, yellow onions, and parsley until coarsely chopped. Add vinegar, ketchup, tomato paste, Creole mustard, horseradish, Worcestershire sauce, salt, pepper, and Tabasco® sauce. Process until finely chopped. Scrape down sides often. With processor running, pour oil in a slow, steady stream, processing until emulsified (or no streaks of oil remain). Mixture should not be pureed but rather uniformly chopped with small bits remaining.

2. Pour into a glass or ceramic bowl. Cover and chill at least 6 hours.

Continued...

CREOLE SHRIMP COCKTAIL
continued...

Assembly:

1. Place lettuce leaves in the bottom of cocktail glasses. Layer in about 1/3 cup (75 mL) Creole sauce to each glass and hang 6 cooked, chilled shrimp on the edge of the glass. Garnish with freshly chopped parsley.

Serves: 6

BRUSCHETTA WITH MARINATED PORTOBELLO MUSHROOMS

Successful marketing has made the giant portobello (or portabella) mushroom very desirable. It is simply a fully mature crimino mushroom, a variety of the common white mushroom. It has a more earthy flavour than most mushrooms and its size makes it very versatile, from serving as a dramatic mock pizza crust to adding delightful flavour to soups. However you use it, remove the inner veins carefully with a spoon – they're somewhat bitter and can add an unpleasant dark colour to foods. Remove the tough woody stem as well, which can be chopped and added to vegetable stocks.

2 large portobello mushrooms, stems and veins removed

1 tablespoon (15 mL) extra virgin olive oil, plus more for brushing mushrooms

2 tablespoons (30 mL) fresh lemon juice

2 garlic cloves, finely minced

1 teaspoon (5 mL) finely chopped fresh rosemary

1 teaspoon (5 mL) chopped fresh thyme leaves

2 tablespoons (30 mL) chopped fresh parsley

Salt and freshly ground black pepper, to taste

10-12 shaved slices of Parmesan cheese, optional

1 loaf sourdough baguette, sliced 1/2 inch (1 cm) thick

4 fresh garlic cloves

About 1 tablespoon (15 mL) extra virgin olive oil

1. Preheat broiler to low. Brush mushrooms on both sides with olive oil. Place rounded side down on a baking sheet and broil for 4-6 minutes, until lightly browned. Remove; let cool until able to handle and then slice into 1/4 inch (0.5 cm) strips. Place in a medium glass or ceramic mixing bowl.

2. Add 1 tablespoon (15 mL) olive oil, lemon juice, garlic, rosemary, thyme, parsley, and salt and pepper to taste.

3. Marinate in the refrigerator for at least two hours.

To serve:

Drain chilled marinated mushroom mixture. Place about 1 tablespoon (15 mL) mushroom mixture on each bruschetta (page 58), top with Parmesan cheese (if using) and serve. On their own, these mushrooms make a great topping for burgers!

Makes: about 12 pieces

MARINATED OLIVES

Kalamata olives are Greek olives that have been marinated in wine vinegar. You can sometimes find them pitted which will be a nice time saver in this recipe. They have a wonderful flavour on their own, but here, combined with a variety of herbs and spices, they are simply divine. This dish would be a wonderful accompaniment to any appetizer buffet table.

2 cups (500 mL) drained and pitted brine-cured black olives, such as Kalamata

2 cups (500 mL) drained and pitted brine-cured green olives

1/4 cup (60 mL) chopped fresh tarragon leaves

1/2 cup (125 mL) chopped fresh basil leaves

4 sprigs fresh thyme

1/2 cup (125 mL) extra virgin olive oil

1/4 cup (60 mL) fresh lemon juice

2 tablespoons (30 mL) minced green onions, white part only

2 tablespoons (30 mL) finely minced garlic

1 tablespoon (15 mL) anise seeds

1 tablespoon (15 mL) fennel seeds

2 teaspoons (10 mL) dried oregano

1 teaspoon (5 mL) dried red chilli flakes

1-2 teaspoons (5-10 mL) freshly ground black pepper

Garnish:

1/2 cup (125 mL) toasted pine nuts

6-8 fresh basil leaves

2-4 tablespoons (30-60 mL) balsamic vinegar

1. In large glass or ceramic mixing bowl, combine all ingredients except garnish.
2. Cover and refrigerate. Marinate at least 6 hours and up to 3 days.
3. To serve, remove thyme sprigs. Transfer to serving dish with slotted spoon. Sprinkle with toasted pine nuts and fresh basil and drizzle with balsamic vinegar.

Makes: about 5 cups (1.25 L)

GRILLED MEDITERRANEAN VEGETABLE STRATA WITH SUN-DRIED TOMATO VINAIGRETTE

Don't shy away from this recipe because of the number of ingredients or the method. It is not difficult to make, but does take time to prepare and set. Ease your workload by preparing the grilled vegetables and onion mixture a day in advance.

This is a delicious way to get a kaleidoscope of colourful and nutritious vegetables infused with Mediterranean flavours. It is perfect for an afternoon luncheon served with grilled sausages and bread. Alternatively, it also makes a stunning presentation as a cold appetizer for an elegant dinner.

There are many ways to roast red peppers. By using this roasting method, you don't struggle with getting the seeds out of roasted peppers.

2 EACH of red and yellow bell peppers, quartered, cored, and seeds removed

2 medium-length zucchini squash, sliced lengthwise in 1/4-1/2 inch (0.5-1 cm) slices

1-2 tablespoons (15-30 mL) extra virgin olive oil

1-2 tablespoons (15-30 mL) butter

1 medium white or yellow onion, thinly sliced

1/2 cup (125 mL) oil-packed sun-dried tomatoes, drained, patted dry, and coarsely chopped

6 garlic cloves, finely minced

1 teaspoon (5 mL) each dried oregano, basil, and freshly ground black pepper

1/2 teaspoon (2.5 mL) salt

1 tablespoon (15 mL) balsamic vinegar

14 ounce (398 mL) can artichoke hearts, drained and each sliced crosswise into thirds

1 3/4 cups (425 mL) tomato juice or blended vegetable juice

2 tablespoons (30 mL) powdered gelatin

Fresh basil leaves (for garnish)

Toasted pine nuts (for garnish)

1. Preheat broiler to low. Place quartered peppers skin side up on a baking sheet and place under the broiler until the skins are blackened. Transfer to a large bowl and cover with plastic wrap to trap the steam. When cool, remove and discard blackened skins.

2. Place zucchini squash slices on a non-stick baking sheet. Lightly brush each side with olive oil. Place under a preheated broiler and cook 3-4 minutes on each side until lightly golden. Cool before use.

Continued...

GRILLED MEDITERRANEAN VEGETABLE STRATA WITH SUN-DRIED TOMATO VINAIGRETTE

continued...

3. Melt butter in a saucepan over medium high heat, add onions and sauté until limp. Add the sun-dried tomatoes, garlic, oregano, basil, pepper, salt, and balsamic vinegar. Continue to cook on a medium heat until onions are caramelized and mixture is thick, about 15 minutes. Remove from heat and set aside.

4. Pour tomato or vegetable juice into a saucepan; add gelatin and heat gently till warm and gelatin has dissolved. Remove and set aside.

5. Line a 5 cup (1.25 L) terrine mould with plastic wrap, ensuring the wrap extends over the sides. Starting with red peppers, line the bottom of the mould, skin side down. Pour in 1/4 of the gelatin mixture, then layer with zucchini squash, artichoke slices, onion mixture, and finish with yellow peppers (skin side up), adding gelatin mixture after each layer. When finished layering, fold the plastic wrap over the mould and press down. Cover and refrigerate until set, about 12 hours.

6. To serve, unmould and slice into 1 inch (2.5 cm) thick slices. Drizzle with Sun-dried Tomato Vinaigrette and garnish with fresh basil leaves and toasted pine nuts.

Serves: 8-10

Sun-Dried Tomato Vinaigrette:

4 oil-packed sun-dried tomatoes, drained and finely chopped

1/4 cup (60 mL) balsamic vinegar

1/2 cup (125 mL) extra virgin olive oil

4 garlic cloves, finely minced

Combine all ingredients and whisk well. Season with salt and pepper.

Makes: 3/4 cup (175 mL)

INDONESIAN SATAY

Satay is a dish native to Indonesia where meat is typically sliced, marinated, and then threaded on skewers and broiled or grilled. It's served with a hot spicy peanut sauce. The peanut sauce here is made simple with the use of peanut butter; make it as hot as you like with the chilli flakes! Theory claims that people in hot climates eat hot food because it causes you to perspire; when beads of sweat accumulate on your skin, any breeze that blows over will have a cooling effect.

Be sure to soak the bamboo skewers in water prior to use so that they don't burn or catch fire under the broiler. You can add flavour, interest, and colour to the skewers by adding chunks of pineapple and red pepper or other favourite vegetables.

1 1/2 pounds (750 g) thick cut (about 1 inch [2.5 cm] thick) sirloin steak, cut into 1/8 inch (0.25 cm) strips (this works best if the meat is still slightly frozen)

3/4 cup (175 mL) soy sauce

1/2 cup (125 mL) lightly packed brown sugar

2 tablespoons (30 mL) vegetable oil

4 garlic cloves, finely minced

1 inch (2.5 cm) piece fresh ginger root, finely minced

24, 6 inch (15 cm) bamboo skewers, soaked in water for 1/2 hour

1. In a medium glass or ceramic mixing bowl, mix all ingredients, except skewers. Cover with plastic wrap and refrigerate. Marinate 4-12 hours.

2. Preheat broiler to low. Thread 1 or 2 pieces of meat on each skewer. Broil until medium rare, about 3-4 minutes.

3. Serve hot with Peanut Sauce.

Makes: 24-30 skewers

Peanut Sauce:

1/4 cup (60 mL) smooth peanut butter

1/3 cup (75 mL) water

2 tablespoons (30 mL) lightly packed brown sugar

1 tablespoon (15 mL) each soy sauce and lemon juice

1 teaspoon (5 mL) red pepper flakes (or more, to taste)

2 garlic cloves, finely minced

1. In a small saucepan, combine all ingredients until well blended. Bring to a boil and then reduce heat and simmer for 5 minutes. Remove from heat. Refrigerate until ready to use

Makes: 2/3 cup

ROASTED EGGPLANT AND RED PEPPER ANTIPASTO WITH FRESH HERBS

Antipasto means 'before the pasta' and refers to any appetizer dish served before a pasta course. This flavourful blend will truly get your appetite ready for what's next on the menu. You could also add a wedge of cheese, sliced Italian salamis, a glass of wine, and have this as a light Friday night dinner.

1 large eggplant, peeled

2 EACH red, yellow, and orange bell peppers, roasted (page 64), de-veined, seeded, and cut into 1/4 inch (0.5 cm) strips

2 jalapeno peppers, de-veined, seeded, and finely chopped

4 garlic cloves, finely minced

1/2 cup (125 mL) drained, pitted, and coarsely chopped Kalamata olives

1/2 cup (125 mL) drained and coarsely chopped pimiento stuffed, brine-cured green olives

1/4 cup (60 mL) EACH chopped fresh parsley, basil, and thyme

1 tablespoon (15 mL) dried oregano leaves

1/4 cup (60 mL) red or white wine vinegar

Salt and freshly ground black pepper, to taste

2 tablespoons (30 mL) extra virgin olive oil, plus extra for brushing eggplant

1. Preheat oven to 500°F (260°C). Line a large baking sheet with parchment paper and set aside.

2. Slice the eggplant into 1/4 inch (0.5 cm) thick slices. Brush with olive oil. Season with salt and pepper. Place on baking sheet and bake for 10-12 minutes, or until lightly browned, turning once. Remove from oven and set aside to cool. When cooled, cut into thin strips.

3. In a large glass or ceramic mixing bowl, combine eggplant strips, roasted peppers, jalapeno peppers, garlic, olives, herbs, and vinegar. Stir gently; season to taste with salt and pepper. Add 2 tablespoons (30 mL) olive oil and stir gently.

4. Cover and refrigerate for 4-8 hours. Serve with sliced ciabatta bread or crostini.

Makes: about 3 cups (750 mL)

SIMPLE OLIVE TAPENADE

Classic tapenade, which hails from the Provence region of France, is a thick paste made from anchovies, ripe olives, capers, olive oil, lemon juice, and sometimes tuna. I've left out the anchovies to reduce the salt and added sun-dried tomatoes for colour and flavour.

1 1/2 cups (375 mL) drained and pitted brine cured, Kalamata olives

1/2 cup (125 mL) drained, pimiento stuffed green olives

1/4 cup (60 mL) drained capers

4 garlic cloves, finely minced

Juice of 1 lemon

Zest of 1 lemon, finely minced

1/2 cup (125 mL) drained, oil packed sun-dried tomatoes

1/4-1/3 cup (60-75 mL) olive oil

2 tablespoons (30 mL) balsamic vinegar

1 chipotle pepper (in adobo sauce), optional

Salt and freshly ground black pepper, to taste

1. Combine all ingredients except salt and pepper in a food processor. Pulse 4-6 times so that mixture forms a thick paste, but is not puréed.

2. Season with salt and pepper.

3. Serve with crostini or other flatbread.

Makes: about 2 cups (500 mL)

SPICED TZATZIKI DIP

Traditionally made from thick, rich sheep's milk yogurt, this tangy sauce is part of the appetizer table in every Greek tavern. To get the same thick, rich texture from cow's milk yogurt, make yogurt cheese as described here. Be sure the yogurt does not contain gelatin or else the liquid will not drain off.

This is also a perfect accompaniment to Pork Souvlaki (page 88) and delicious as a dip for pita bread wedges.

1 medium field cucumber

2 cups (500 mL) plain yogurt
(to make 1 1/2 cups [375 mL] soft yogurt cheese)

3 garlic cloves, finely minced

2 tablespoons (15 mL) finely chopped fresh mint

1 teaspoon (5 mL) ground cumin

1/2 teaspoon (2.5 mL) toasted sesame oil

1/4 cup (60 mL) toasted sesame seeds

1. Peel the cucumber; slice in half, lengthwise, and remove the seeds with a spoon and discard. Coarsely grate the shelled cucumber with a grater. Place grated cucumber in a strainer set over a bowl and set on the counter for 1-3 hours to allow all the liquid to drain. Squeeze cucumber to remove the last bit of liquid. Discard liquid.

2. At the same time, make the yogurt cheese. Line a strainer set over a bowl with two layers of cheesecloth. Place the yogurt in the cheesecloth; refrigerate for 2 hours; discard the liquid that drains through and you will have soft yogurt cheese left in the cheesecloth.

3. Place grated cucumber in a medium-size mixing bowl. Add yogurt cheese, garlic, mint, cumin, and sesame oil. Stir to combine. Transfer to a serving bowl and sprinkle with sesame seeds.

4. Serve with spiced pita wedges, fresh vegetables, or crackers.

Makes: 2 1/2 cups (625 mL)

STEAMED PRAWN AND SCALLOP RAVIOLI WITH CARROT AND GINGER BROTH

This recipe hails from a chef friend of mine. It's brilliantly simple and the flavours are delicate but sublime. Serve it as a first course for an elegant meal.

Ravioli:

4 medium size prawns, coarsely chopped

6 large scallops, coarsely chopped

1 small carrot, finely diced

2 green onions, white and green part, thinly sliced

2 tablespoons (30 mL) sesame oil

1 inch (2.5 cm) piece fresh ginger, finely diced

Pinch salt and freshly ground white pepper

1 egg, slightly beaten

8 large wonton wrappers

2 finely sliced green onions, for garnish

Carrot and Ginger Broth:

4 cups (1 L) vegetable or chicken broth

2 coarsely chopped carrots, about 1 cup (250 mL)

1 inch (2.5 cm) piece fresh ginger

For broth:

1. In a medium sauce pan, simmer broth, carrots, and ginger for 25-30 minutes until carrots are tender.
2. Remove from heat and purée with a hand blender or in a food processor until smooth.

Continued...

STEAMED PRAWN AND SCALLOP RAVIOLI WITH CARROT AND GINGER BROTH

continued...

For ravioli:

1. In a medium mixing bowl, combine prawns, scallops, carrot, onions, sesame oil, ginger, and salt and pepper. Stir to combine.

2. To make ravioli, place 1 wonton wrapper on plate. Spoon 1/4 of the seafood mixture on the wrapper. Brush edges with egg. Place another wonton wrapper on top and press edges to seal.

3. Repeat to make 4 ravioli.

4. In a large double boiler steam the ravioli for 5-7 minutes. Remove from heat.

Assembly:

Place 1 cup (250 mL) broth in serving bowl. Top with 1 ravioli. Garnish with finely sliced green onion.

Serves: 4 as a first course

SPICY WHITE BEAN DIP

White kidney beans are also known as cannellini beans, which are often used in Italian dishes. They have a milder flavour than red kidney beans and as such, carry the flavours well of other added recipe ingredients. You can purchase them dried and rehydrate them if you like. To save time, I use canned and rinsed white kidney beans to make this recipe quickly and easily. To reduce the unwanted gas associated with bean intake, rinse the beans and discard the thick liquid from the can.

Tahini is a thick paste made from sesame seeds and is one of the main ingredients of hummus. Here, it adds a lovely nutty flavour.

19-ounce (540 mL) can cannellini beans, drained

1/3 cup (75 mL) olive oil

1 teaspoon (5 mL) sesame oil

1/4 cup (60 mL) fresh lemon juice

1 tablespoon (15 mL) tahini

3 garlic cloves, finely minced

1 teaspoon (5 mL) ground coriander

1/2 teaspoon (2.5 mL) EACH salt and freshly ground white pepper

1 teaspoon (5 mL) ground cumin

1/2 teaspoon (2.5 mL) hot pepper sauce, such as Tabasco®

3 tablespoons (45 mL) chopped cilantro, for garnish

1. Combine all ingredients, except cilantro, in a food processor and process until smooth.

2. Taste and adjust seasoning with salt, pepper, and Tabasco® sauce.

3. When ready to serve, garnish with chopped cilantro. Serve with toasted pita chips or your favourite cracker. This dip can also double as a great spread on sandwiches.

Makes: about 1 1/2 cups (375 mL)

THE MAIN EVENT

The nominees to take centre stage on the dinner table include meat, fish, seafood, poultry and pasta. Generally speaking, the entree is the most costly part of the meal, so you want to be sure you know some of the basics of cooking these protein rich foods. We've all experienced overcooked, tough, or dry beef and pork, leathery chicken, rubbery shrimp, and gummy pasta. But it doesn't ever have to happen as long as you know some cooking basics.

As protein rich foods cook, the fibres start to shorten. Knowing the ideal time to stop the cooking process will guarantee a safely cooked, tender and juicy product. Here are the basics:

- Use the right type of cooking method for the item being cooked. Dry heat methods include baking, broiling, roasting and grilling. Generally speaking, foods that are more tender at the start lend themselves well to this type of cooking method. Foods such as beef sirloin steaks, rib roasts, pork loin roasts, pork tenderloin, lamb chops, whole chicken, chicken parts, all types of fish, and most shellfish do well with dry heat cooking methods. Foods, however, that are tough at the start, need a little help through the cooking process to make them more tender. Items such as beef chuck, blade, flank or shank come from the part of the animal that moves a lot and, as a result, the muscles are very tough. These items are best cooked by moist heat methods such as stewing or braising. The long cooking process and the addition of various liquids help to tenderize the meat and produce a delicious, juicy final product.

- Cook the food to the proper internal temperature (using a meat thermometer is best) to ensure it is safe. Overcooked meat, fish, and poultry can become dry and tough.

- Carve the item properly. This applies mostly to roasts and flank steak. Be sure to cut across the grain (or fibres) of the meat and not along the grain line. This will help ensure a tender product.

- Practice a few times – that's the best way to gain confidence in cooking your ideal Main Event!

APRICOT STUFFED ROAST PORK LOIN WITH ROSEMARY GLAZE

I just love how the flavours of shallots, garlic, apricots, and rosemary meld to make this roast a show stopper.

3-4-pound (1.5-2 kg) boned, rolled, and tied centre pork loin roast

2 tablespoons (30 mL) butter

1/2 cup (125 mL) finely chopped shallots

3/4 cup (175 mL) finely chopped dried apricots

2 tablespoons (30 mL) finely chopped parsley

1/2 cup (125 mL) fresh breadcrumbs (from 1-2 slices fresh bread, crumbled between your fingers)

1/2 teaspoon (2.5 mL) EACH salt and freshly ground black pepper

1 tablespoon (15 mL) vegetable oil

1. Preheat oven to 375°F (190°C).

2. In a medium skillet, melt butter and sauté shallots for 3-4 minutes. Add apricots, parsley, breadcrumbs, and salt and pepper, and cook for 1-2 minutes more. Remove from heat and cool thoroughly.

3. Untie and unroll pork loin roast. Spread stuffing over roast; roll and re-tie.

4. In a Dutch oven, heat 1 tablespoon (15 mL) vegetable oil over medium-high heat. Add pork roast and brown on all sides.

5. Place in oven for about 1- 1 1/2 hours or until internal temperature registers 160°F (71°C). Let rest 15 minutes before slicing. Serve with Apricot Rosemary Glaze. Serve with scalloped potatoes and Roasted Veggies with Soy and Garlic (page 156).

Serves: 8

Continued...

APRICOT STUFFED ROAST PORK LOIN WITH ROSEMARY GLAZE
continued...

Apricot Rosemary Glaze:

2 tablespoons (30 mL) olive oil

4 garlic cloves, finely minced

2/3 cup (150 mL) apricot jam

2 tablespoons (30 mL) balsamic vinegar

2 sprigs fresh rosemary

Salt and freshly ground black pepper

1. In a small saucepan, heat olive oil over medium heat. Add garlic and sauté until flavour is released but do not let the garlic turn brown. Add the remaining ingredients and cook until heated through. Remove from heat. Refrigerate until ready to use. Reheat and remove rosemary sprigs before service. Season with salt and pepper.

Makes: 2/3 cup (150 mL)

BEEF STEW WITH MERLOT, MUSHROOMS, AND PEARL ONIONS

Similar to braising, stewing uses moist heat to tenderize tough cuts of meat. Typically when stewing, smaller cuts of meat are used such as in this recipe. The stewing liquid is where much of the flavour comes from. Using a good quality Merlot wine together with a rich broth, tomatoes, mushrooms, and onions produces a delicious stew. Serve this stew over cooked egg noodles or steamed brown rice.

When selecting a cooking wine, a good rule of thumb is to 'only cook with wine that you will drink'. It doesn't have to be an expensive wine, but certainly one that you would be pleased to drink.

1 1/2 cups (375 mL) Merlot wine

2 tablespoons (30 mL) chopped garlic

1 teaspoon (5 mL) salt

1 teaspoon (5 mL) ground black pepper

2 pounds (about 1 kg) beef stew meat, cut into 1 inch (2.5 cm) pieces

2 tablespoons (30 mL) vegetable oil

1/4 cup (60 mL) all-purpose flour

1 tablespoon (15 mL) tomato paste

Reserved marinade from above

1/2 cup (125 mL) canned whole tomatoes, drained

3 cups (750 mL) beef stock or broth

2 tablespoons (30 mL) butter

1/2 pound (250 g) white mushrooms, cut into quarters

10 ounce (284 g) package frozen pearl onions, defrosted and drained

6 slices bacon, cut into 1 inch (2.5 cm) pieces

1. In a large glass or ceramic bowl, combine wine, garlic, salt, pepper, and beef. Stir to combine. Cover and refrigerate for 12-24 hours. Turn occasionally to make sure all the beef is well marinated.

2. Preheat oven to 350°F (180°C).

3. Strain beef and reserve marinade. Dry the beef with a paper towel.

4. In a large oven-proof saucepot or Dutch oven, heat the vegetable oil. Add the beef in small batches and brown on all sides. As the beef is browned, strain it and remove to a warm plate. Once all the beef is cooked, add it back to the saucepot and sprinkle it with flour; stir and cook for about 2 minutes.

Continued...

BEEF STEW WITH MERLOT, MUSHROOMS, AND PEARL ONIONS
continued...

5. Add the tomato paste, stir, and cook for another 3 minutes. Add the reserved marinade, canned tomatoes, and stock or broth. Bring to a boil and boil for 10 minutes.

6. Cover and cook in preheated oven for 2 1/2 – 3 hours or until beef is very tender. Remove from the oven.

7. In a small saucepan, melt butter over medium-high heat. Add mushrooms and sauté 5-7 minutes. Add to the meat mixture. In the same saucepan, cook the bacon until semi-crisp. Add to meat mixture along with the drained pearl onions. Return to the oven and cook for an additional 30 minutes until flavours are blended.

Optional: This stew will have a very thin sauce. If you prefer a thicker sauce, you can thicken it with a cornstarch slurry. A slurry is a combination of starch and a cool liquid. To make a cornstarch slurry, in a small cup or bowl, dissolve 2 tablespoons (30 mL) cornstarch in 1/2 cup (125 mL) COLD water. Stir to dissolve. Add the slurry to the hot stew mixture and stir to combine. Return to oven and cook for an additional 15 minutes, stirring often.

Serves: 4-6

BIKER JOHN'S RIBS

This recipe comes from a dear friend of mine who was born in the Southern US. He once took me for a ride (at great speed!) on his Harley-Davidson motorcycle – now there's a thrill! Coming home to grilled ribs after a ride like that made the day pretty special.

6 racks baby back ribs, cut into 3-4 rib portions

Sauce:

3 bottles, 15 ounces (425 mL) each of purchased hickory-flavoured barbeque sauce

1/2 cup (125 mL) orange juice concentrate

1/2 cup (125 mL) lemon juice

12 garlic cloves, finely minced

1/2 cup (125 mL) Worcestershire sauce

2 teaspoons (10 mL) Tabasco® sauce

1/2 cup (125 mL) molasses

1/2 cup (125 mL) lightly packed brown sugar

For sauce:

1. Combine all sauce ingredients in a large pot. Bring to a boil and then simmer for 30 minutes. Season with salt and freshly ground black pepper. Refrigerate until ready to use.

For ribs:

1. Place rib portions in large pot of boiling water. Bring to a boil, reduce heat, and simmer for about 1 hour or until meat pulls easily away from the bone. Remove ribs and place on clean, dry baking sheets.

2. Preheat oven to 300°F (150°C). Coat ribs generously with sauce. Cover with aluminum foil and bake in preheated oven for 1 hour. Remove from oven.

3. Heat grill to medium-low. Place ribs on grill and baste with cooked sauce until ribs glisten, about 20-30 minutes.

Serve with Backyard Potato Salad (page 144).

Serves: 10-12, depending on how hungry you are!

BLACKENED STEAK SALAD WITH SALSA AND BLACK BEANS

This steak can be prepared on the outdoor grill, or alternatively, broiled in the oven to desired doneness. It's perfect on a hot summer evening. Add a crusty French baguette to complement the meal.

1 pound (500 g) thickly cut strip sirloin steaks trimmed of visible fat

1 tablespoon (15 mL) commercially prepared Cajun spice mixture

1 cup (250 mL) prepared salsa, hot or mild

1/2 cup (125 mL) sour cream, full or fat-reduced

1/2 cup (125 mL) prepared or home prepared guacamole

1 cup (250 mL) canned black beans, drained

1/2 cup (125 mL) home prepared or purchased roasted red peppers

4 cups (1 L) mesclun salad green mix or washed and trimmed baby spinach

2 fresh limes, cut in half

1. Preheat grill to medium high heat (or preheat broiler to high). Season steak with Cajun spice on both sides. Grill to medium rare. Remove from heat and set aside to rest for 5-7 minutes.

2. Place 1 cup (250 mL) salad greens on each of 4 dinner plates. Top each plate attractively with 1/4 cup (60 mL) salsa, 2 tablespoons (30 mL) sour cream, 2 tablespoons (30 mL) guacamole, 1/4 cup (60 mL) black beans, and 2 tablespoons (30 mL) roasted red pepper.

3. Slice steak thinly across grain. Place steak slices atop each salad. Sprinkle with fresh lime juice and serve.

Serves: 4

HERB-CRUSTED TENDERLOIN OF BEEF

This is one of my very favourite recipes. I just love the tenderness of this prime cut of beef, and the infusion of flavours in the crust makes it a winner with dinner guests. This is an expensive meal so take care in preparing and cooking the beef.

Silver skin is a very, very tough membrane present on beef tenderloin (and some other meat cuts as well such as pork tenderloin) and must be removed with a sharp knife before cooking the meat. If you don't, this expensive and normally extremely tender cut of meat will have a chewy, tough exterior and you won't be pleased! You can recognize silver skin by its silvery opaque colour.

2 1/2 - 3 pound (1.25-1.5 kg) beef tenderloin, trimmed of fat and silver skin

1/3 cup (75 mL) very soft butter

1/2 cup (125 mL) finely minced fresh parsley

1/4 cup (60 mL) EACH finely minced fresh rosemary and thyme

8 garlic cloves, finely minced

1 teaspoon (5 mL) salt

2 tablespoons (30 mL) freshly ground black pepper

1/4 cup (60 mL) Dijon mustard

3/4 cup (175 mL) fine dry breadcrumbs

1/4 cup (60 mL) Worcestershire sauce

1/2 cup (125 mL) water (more or less as needed)

1. In a medium mixing bowl, combine butter, herbs, garlic, salt, pepper, mustard, breadcrumbs, and Worcestershire sauce. Add enough water to make a medium-thick paste.

2. Spread paste thinly and evenly over the entire tenderloin.

3. If present, tuck thinner end of tenderloin underneath, so that it will cook evenly. Place tenderloin on a rack in a roasting pan.

4. Roast by one of the following methods:

Continued...

HERB-CRUSTED TENDERLOIN OF BEEF

continued...

When you look at the entire tenderloin, it's not an even muscle – there is a larger end called the 'butt tenderloin' which then narrows down to the smaller end or 'short tenderloin'. You want the meat to cook evenly, so if you have the short tenderloin on your cut of beef, be sure to tuck it under the middle of the meat to produce a roast that's even in appearance and will cook evenly. The middle part of a whole tenderloin is the most tender and where you get the 'chateaubriand' roast or filet mignon steaks from.

For a crispy crust:

Preheat oven to 525°F (275°C). Place tenderloin in oven and immediately reduce heat to 375°F (190°C). Roast to desired doneness. This method will produce a crispy crust and the ends will be more 'well done' than the centre.

For an evenly cooked roast:

Preheat oven to 300°F (150°C). Place tenderloin in oven and cooked to desired doneness, as above. This method will yield a very tender roast that is evenly cooked throughout, but lacks a crispy crust.

A note on 'desired doneness'. To serve a beef roast at medium rare, the final internal temperature should be 140°F (60°C). To serve a beef roast at medium, it should be 150°F (65°C). Most roasts should 'rest' after removed from the oven, tented with aluminum foil to keep warm, for about 15 minutes so that the juices can return to the inner part of the meat, making a juicy roast. So, if you cook the roast to the desired doneness in the oven, it will be overcooked by the time you serve it-during that 15 minutes of resting, it continues to cook by what's called carry-over cooking. So, if I want my roast at medium rare, I often remove it from the oven at 130°F (50°C); this way, during the carry-over cooking process, it will reach the desired internal serving temperature. You may have to experiment a couple of times to get it right. However, I would suggest experimenting on a less expensive cut of roast such as inside round.

Serve with Almond Rice Pilaf with Lemon and Thyme (page 136) and Sautéed Mushrooms with Shallots and Fresh Thyme (page 157).

Serves: 6-8 depending on portion size

JAMMIN' PORK TENDERLOIN

This sauce has it all – sweet, spicy, and tangy all at once. When I first made this dish, my children went crazy over it, and it's become a household favourite. Serve with a rice pilaf studded with apricots and raisins and some steamed broccoli for a beautiful weeknight supper.

One of the classic errors home cooks make in browning meat is to turn it too often. Browning takes time. If you start with hot oil and brown the meat for several minutes, you'll get the nice brown caramelized look on the meat. Be sure to brown all sides of the meat.

1 whole pork tenderloin, about 1 1/2 pounds (750 g) trimmed of silver skin

Salt and pepper

About 1/2 cup (125 mL) all-purpose flour

1 large egg, lightly whisked with 1 tablespoon (15 mL) water

About 1/2 cup (125 mL) fine, dry bread crumbs

1-2 tablespoons (15-30 mL) olive oil

1/3 cup (75 mL) chicken broth

1/3 cup (75 mL) sherry

2 tablespoons (30 mL) jalapeno pepper jelly

2 tablespoons (30 mL) apricot jam

2 tablespoons (30 mL) ginger marmalade

1. On a clean cutting board, slice the pork tenderloin into 3/4 inch (1.5 cm) medallions; flatten slightly with the heel of your hand to 1/2 inch (1 cm). You should get 10-12 medallions from a medium-sized pork tenderloin.

2. Prepare a simple breading station: put the flour, egg/water, and bread crumbs into each of 3 small bowls.

3. Season pork medallions with salt and pepper. Dip each first into flour (shake off excess), then into egg/water mixture, and finally into bread crumbs (shake off); place on clean platter.

4. Heat a 10 inch (25 cm) skillet to medium high heat and add olive oil. Swirl to coat pan. When oil is medium hot (be sure the meat 'sizzles' when you add it), add 4-5 medallions and sauté for 3-4 minutes or until bottoms are golden brown. Turn over and sauté additional 3-4 minutes. Remove and transfer to warm plate. Repeat with remaining medallions.

Continued...

JAMMIN' PORK TENDERLOIN
continued...

5. When finished cooking medallions, in the same skillet, increase the heat to high; deglaze the pan with the broth and sherry, being sure to scrape up the brown bits from the pan. Reduce slightly (about 1-2 minutes). Add all 3 jellies and stir to dissolve and combine. Return medallions to the skillet and cook for an additional 5-7 minutes or until only a slight pink remains in the centre and the sauce is thick and bubbling. Remove from heat and serve.

Serve with baked sweet potatoes and Pan-Steamed Spinach with Garlic and Sesame Seeds (page 155).

Serves: 4-6

SPICED LAMB BURGERS WITH MINT AND CILANTRO

These delightful burgers have a wonderful unique flavour. I've found the secret to tasty and juicy burgers is to stir the ingredients until just combined and be gentle when forming the burgers. If you mix them too well and compress them too tightly when forming, the texture will be more like a meatloaf than a juicy burger.

1 pound (500 g) ground lamb
4 garlic cloves, finely minced
1/2 cup (125 mL) finely minced red onion
1 large egg
2 teaspoons (10 mL) dried mint leaves
1 tablespoon (15 mL) finely chopped fresh cilantro
2 jalapeno peppers, seeded and finely chopped
1 inch (2.5 cm) piece ginger root, finely grated
1 teaspoon (5 mL) ground cumin
1 teaspoon (5 mL) ground white pepper
1/2 teaspoon (2.5 mL) ground cayenne pepper
1 teaspoon (5 mL) salt

1. In a large mixing bowl, combine all ingredients. Stir gently to combine but do not over mix.
2. Form into 4 inch (10 cm) wide by 1 inch (2.5 cm) thick patties.
3. On a preheated grill, grill until desired doneness, at least medium rare.
4. Alternatively, the mixture can be wrapped around metal skewers, about 1 inch (2.5 cm) thick and 4-5 inches (10-13 cm) long and grilled. Remove from skewers after cooking and place in pita pockets and serve with feta cheese and purchased hummus.

Serve on whole grain hamburger buns and top with feta cheese and purchased hummus or Spiced Tzatziki Dip (page 69).

Serves: 4

LAMB CHILLI WITH BLACK BEANS

When I speak of cooking lamb, a few people get a really big smile on their face, but many cringe. I grew up eating lamb – really good baby or spring lamb-and I still love it. But I think many people had the misfortune of eating mutton in the past and now associate this with baby lamb. Baby lamb and spring lamb are very young animals and have a very delicate flavour and tender flesh. Mutton is lamb that is over two years old and, with age, has developed a strong flavour and tough flesh. If you want to give lamb a try again, try it in this chilli, where the flavour is more subtle. If you prefer, you can substitute ground beef for the lamb. This chilli is even better the next day.

2 tablespoons (30 mL) olive oil

2 pounds (1 kg) ground lamb

1 cup (250 mL) finely diced red onion

6 garlic cloves, finely minced

2 tablespoons (30 mL) chilli powder

1 tablespoon (15 mL) dried oregano

1 tablespoon (15 mL) ground cumin

1 tablespoon (15 mL) ground coriander

3 cups (750 mL) chicken broth or stock

1 28-ounce can (796 mL) crushed tomatoes

2 tablespoons (30 mL) Worcestershire sauce

2 tablespoons (30 mL) tomato paste

1 teaspoon (5 mL) EACH salt and freshly ground black pepper

19-ounce can (540 mL) black beans, rinsed and drained

1/4 cup (60 mL) chopped cilantro, for garnish

1/2 cup (125 mL) sour cream, for garnish

1. In a large pot, heat olive oil and brown ground lamb until no pink remains. Drain off all but 1 tablespoon (15 mL) of fat and discard. Remove lamb to a small bowl and keep warm.

2. Add onion, garlic, chilli powder, oregano, cumin, and coriander to the pot. Stir well to combine and sauté 3-4 minutes. Add broth, tomatoes, Worcestershire sauce, tomato paste, salt, pepper and cooked lamb. Mix well. Bring to a boil; cover, reduce heat and simmer for 1 1/2 – 2 hours.

3. Add black beans, stir and cover to simmer for an additional 30 minutes.

4. Garnish with sour cream and chopped cilantro.

Serve with Cheesy Jalapeno Cornmeal Muffins (page 5)
Serves: 8

MARINATED FLANK STEAK WITH MUSTARD SAUCE

Flank steak is so poorly understood and gets so little respect. The flank is located on the lower side of the belly of the cow. It has quite a bit of fat and connective tissue (tissues that hold together muscles) and is full of flavour if cooked properly. Because it's so tough, flank steak works great if first tenderized with a flavourful marinade. Then, it's best grilled over high heat just until medium rare – anything more and it quickly turns very tough.

1 tablespoon (15 mL) olive oil

1 cup (250 mL) finely chopped onion

2 garlic cloves, finely minced

1 teaspoon (5 mL) EACH curry powder, chilli powder, and black pepper

3/4 cup (175 mL) soy sauce

3 tablespoons (45 mL) honey

1/3 cup (75 mL) olive oil

1/3 cup (75 mL) fresh lime juice

1 flank steak, about 2 pounds (about 1 kg)

1. In a large skillet, heat 1 tablespoon (15 mL) olive oil and sauté onions until soft, about 3-4 minutes. Add garlic and sauté for one minute more.

2. Add curry powder, chilli powder, and black pepper, and sauté an additional 2 minutes.

3. Add soy sauce, honey, 1/3 cup (75 mL) olive oil, and lime juice. Stir to combine. Remove from heat and cool completely in the refrigerator.

4. In a re-sealable plastic bag, place flank steak and add cold marinade.

5. Refrigerate and marinate for 24-48 hours, turning occasionally.

6. On a hot grill, cook meat to medium rare, about 6 minutes per side. Remove from heat and let rest about 3-5 minutes.

7. To serve, slice thinly across the grain and at a diagonal and serve with Mustard Sauce.

Continued...

MARINATED FLANK STEAK WITH MUSTARD SAUCE
continued...

Mustard Sauce:

1 cup (250 mL) sour cream, full or fat-reduced
2 tablespoons (30 mL) Dijon mustard
1 tablespoon (15 mL) soy sauce
1 tablespoon (15 mL) Worcestershire sauce
1 tablespoon (15 mL) finely chopped onion
Freshly ground pepper, to taste

1. In a small bowl, combine all ingredients and mix well.
2. Refrigerate overnight and serve chilled with flank steak.

Serve with baked potatoes and Sweet Curried Carrots (page 158).

Serves: 6

PORK SOUVLAKI

This pork is bursting with tangy lemon, fragrant garlic, sweet herbs, and spicy chilli. It's a favourite in our household. You can also substitute lamb or chicken for the pork.

2 pounds (1 kg) boneless pork, cut into 1 inch (2.5 cm) cubes from pork shoulder, sirloin chops, or tenderloin

1/3 cup (75 mL) olive oil

5 garlic cloves, finely minced

2 tablespoons (30 mL) fresh lemon juice

1 tablespoon (15 mL) dried oregano

1 tablespoon (15 mL) dried mint leaves

1/2 teaspoon (2.5 mL) salt

1 teaspoon (5 mL) freshly ground black pepper

1 teaspoon (5 mL) dried red chilli flakes

6-8 metal or bamboo skewers (if using bamboo, soak in water for 1 hour prior to use)

2 small red onions, cut into quarters

6 small warm whole wheat pita

Spiced Tzatziki Dip (page 69)

1/2 cup (125 mL) feta cheese

1. In a medium glass or ceramic bowl, combine pork with the next 8 ingredients and mix well. Cover and marinate in the refrigerator for 8-24 hours.

2. Remove meat from marinade. Preheat oven to 425°F (215°C). Thread 3-4 pieces of meat alternately with onions onto skewers. Place on parchment lined baking sheet.

3. Bake in preheated oven for 12-15 minutes or until pork is cooked through. These also work very well cooked on the grill.

To serve, remove meat/onion from skewer and place in warm pita. Top with Spiced Tzatziki Dip (page 69) and sprinkle with crumbled feta cheese.

Serves: 6

Pulled Pork Sandwiches
page 92

Cod with Fragrant Vegetables and Toasted Almonds

page 98

PORK SIRLOIN STEAKS WITH GARLIC ROSEMARY BALSAMIC GLAZE

Here's a simple supper for a weeknight. I really like this cut of pork for quick and simple meals. I find it more juicy and tender than pork chops and the steaks cook quickly.

2 tablespoons (30 mL) olive oil

Salt and freshly ground black pepper

4 boneless, pork sirloin steaks, about 1 1/2 pounds (750 g) total (this cut is often large, so after cooking, the steaks may need to be cut in half)

4 garlic cloves, finely minced

1 tablespoon (15 mL) chopped fresh rosemary

1/2 cup (125 mL) good quality balsamic vinegar

Freshly ground black pepper

1. Preheat oven to 375°F (190°C).

2. Heat oil in a large skillet on medium-high. Season pork steaks with salt and pepper. Working in batches, sear steaks until golden brown, about 2-3 minutes per side. As they are seared, transfer to a large baking dish.

3. In the same skillet, sauté garlic until fragrant, but not brown, about 1-2 minutes. Add rosemary and vinegar and bring to a boil to complete the glaze.

4. Pour the glaze over the pork steaks and bake in preheated oven for 15 minutes or until just a slight trace of pink remains in the centre of the meat. Remove from oven and serve, pouring a little of the glaze over each of the chops.

5. Finish with additional ground black pepper.

Serve atop steamed couscous.

Serves: 6-8

PULLED PORK SANDWICHES

Mention 'pulled pork' and you're immediately into Southern Barbecue. Pulled pork is traditionally made by cooking pork over a low smoky fire until the meat can be pulled apart by hand. There are countless versions of pulled pork with varieties in smokes, sauces, rubs, marinades, and serving styles. Here, to save time, the pork is cooked in a Dutch oven. A Dutch oven is a thick-walled, metal cooking pot, often on three legs, with a tight fitting lid. Modern day Dutch ovens are often coated with enamel. If you don't have a Dutch oven, don't fret – simply use a large heavy pot with a tight fitting lid.

Pork:

4 pounds (2 kg) bone-in, pork butt roast

6 garlic cloves, finely minced

Salt and freshly ground black pepper

1 tablespoon (15 mL) vegetable oil

4 cups (1 L) chicken stock or broth

2 bay leaves

Sauce:

2 tablespoons (30 mL) vegetable oil

1 1/2 cups (375 mL) finely chopped white or yellow onions

5 garlic cloves, finely minced

2 cups (500 mL) ketchup

1 cup (250 mL) commercially prepared chilli sauce

1 cup (250 mL) white wine vinegar

1/2 cup (125 mL) lightly packed brown sugar

1/3 cup (75 mL) Worcestershire sauce

1/4 cup (60 mL) lemon juice

1/4 cup (60 mL) yellow mustard

2 tablespoon (30 mL) molasses

2 teaspoons (10 mL) salt

1-2 teaspoons (5-10 mL) freshly ground black pepper

1-2 teaspoons (5-10 mL) Tabasco® sauce (optional)

Continued...

PULLED PORK SANDWICHES

continued...

For pork:

1. Rub garlic all over pork roast. Season with salt and pepper.

2. In a Dutch oven, heat vegetable oil. Brown pork on all sides. Add chicken stock or broth and bay leaf. Bring stock to a boil and then reduce to a simmer. Simmer, covered for about 3 hours, turning meat occasionally and being sure the liquid does not evaporate.

For sauce:

1. In a large saucepan, heat oil and sauté onions until soft, about 5 minutes. Add garlic and sauté an additional 2 minutes. Add remaining ingredients and bring to a boil.

2. Reduce to a simmer and cook for about 30 minutes. Season with salt and pepper if necessary. Remove from heat; cool and refrigerate until ready to use.

Assembly:

1. When meat is fully cooked, remove meat from broth and let cool slightly. "Pull" the pork apart and add to simmering sauce. Discard broth.

2. Simmer for an additional 1 hour until meat is well infused with sauce flavours.

3. Serve open-face over whole grain crusty buns or warm mashed potatoes.

Serves: 8-10

PORK MEDALLIONS WITH RED ONION CHUTNEY

To make this dish in a flash, make the chutney a day or two in advance. Simply reheat it to serving temperature when ready to serve the pork medallions.

Pork:

1 whole pork tenderloin, about 1 1/2 pounds (750 g) trimmed of silver skin

Salt and pepper

About 1/2 cup (125 mL) flour

1 large egg, lightly whisked with 1 tablespoon (15 mL) water

About 1/2 cup (125 mL) fine bread crumbs

1-2 tablespoons (15-30 mL) olive oil

Chutney:

1 tablespoon (15 mL) vegetable oil

1 tablespoon (15 mL) butter

2 medium red onions, very finely sliced

1 tablespoon (15 mL) lemon juice

1/4 cup (60 mL) red wine vinegar

2 tablespoons (30 mL) honey

1 tablespoon (15 mL) balsamic vinegar

1 bay leaf

1/2 teaspoon (2.5 mL) whole caraway seeds

Salt and pepper to taste

For pork:

1. On a clean cutting board, slice the pork tenderloin into 3/4 inch (1.5 cm) medallions; flatten slightly with the heel of your hand to 1/2 inch (1 cm). You should have 10-12 medallions from a medium pork tenderloin.

2. Prepare a simple breading station: put the flour, egg/water and bread crumbs into each of 3 small bowls.

Continued...

PORK MEDALLIONS WITH RED ONION CHUTNEY
continued...

3. Season pork medallions with salt and pepper. Dip each first into flour (shake off excess), then into egg/water mixture, and finally into bread crumbs (shake off); place on clean platter.

4. Heat a 10 inch (25 cm) skillet to medium high heat and add olive oil. Swirl to coat pan. When oil is medium hot, add 4-5 medallions (be sure they 'sizzle' so you know the pan is hot enough) and sauté for 3-4 minutes or until bottoms are golden brown. Turn over and finish cooking until only a slight trace of pink remains in the centre of the pork. As medallions are cooked, remove to serving dish and keep warm. Finish cooking remaining medallions.

5. Serve warm chutney atop each pork medallion.

For chutney:

1. In a large skillet, heat oil and butter until melted. Add onions and cook 3-4 minutes until they start to wilt. Add lemon juice, red wine vinegar, honey, balsamic vinegar, bay leaf, and caraway seeds. Cook over medium heat until mixture is thick and syrupy, about 15-20 minutes. Stir occasionally. Season to taste with salt and pepper. Remove bay leaf prior to service.

Serve each cooked pork medallion topped with 1 tablespoon (15 mL) chutney. Serve with roast potatoes and Pan-Steamed Spinach with Garlic and Sesame Seeds (page 155).

Serves: 4-6

RIB EYE STEAKS WITH BRANDIED PEPPERCORN SAUCE

It's time for a lesson in peppercorns. Peppercorns are a spice grown in berry-like clusters on the pepper plant native to India and Indonesia. There are 3 types of peppercorns produced from the pepper berry: white, black, and green. White peppercorns are derived from the ripest berries; their outer skin is removed and the remaining berry is dried. Black peppercorns are the most widely used worldwide. Here the berries are picked when they are not quite ripe and allowed to shrivel and dry, producing a strong spicy flavour. Green peppercorns are immature and soft berries, which are often brined and then canned, the type used in this recipe. Pink peppercorns aren't peppercorns at all but rather dried berries from a rose plant native to Madagascar.

1/4 cup (60 mL) butter

1/2 cup (125 mL) finely minced shallots

1/4 cup (60 mL) drained, brined peppercorns
[1/2 of 7 ounce (212 mL) can]

2 tablespoons (30 mL) brandy or Cognac

1/2 cup (125 mL) whipping cream

6 rib eye steaks, each 1/2 – 3/4 inch (1-1.5 cm) thick

1. In a medium sauce pan, heat butter and sauté shallots until soft, but not brown.
2. Add peppercorns and heat thoroughly, breaking up peppercorns with the back of a spoon as you stir.
3. Add brandy or Cognac and heat for another 1-2 minutes.
4. Add cream and reduce slightly to make a thick peppercorn sauce.
5. Meanwhile, season steaks with salt and pepper. On a hot grill, cook to desired doneness. Remove and let rest for 5 minutes. Serve with peppercorn sauce.

Serves: 6

BAKED HALIBUT WITH PERNOD SAUCE

Halibut is a firm fleshed, mild flavoured, large white fish native to the northern Atlantic and Pacific oceans. Halibut steaks are cut across the fish leaving the bone in the centre, whereas fillets are boneless. Halibut nicely takes on the flavours of other ingredients being cooked with it and can handle both mild and stronger flavours. Here, the light flavour of Pernod, a licorice-flavoured liqueur found in most liquor stores, is a wonderful accompanying flavour. On a curious chemistry note, when Pernod is combined with water, it turns white and cloudy.

6 halibut fillets or steaks (1 1/2 pounds [750g] total) boneless, skinless, and trimmed

1 tablespoon (15 mL) commercial lemon pepper spice mixture

Sauce:

2 tablespoons (30 mL) butter

1/2 cup (125 mL) finely minced shallots

2 garlic cloves, finely minced

1/2 cup (125 mL) dry white wine

1/4 cup (60 mL) Pernod

1/3 cup (75 mL) chicken stock or broth

1/3 cup (75 mL) whipping cream

Salt and freshly ground white pepper, to taste

Finely chopped fresh parsley and/or cilantro for garnish

For fish:

1. Preheat oven to 400°F (200°C).

2. Sprinkle each side of the fish with lemon pepper spice mixture. Place fish pieces on baking sheet and bake in preheated oven until cooked through, about 10-15 minutes depending on the thickness of the fish. Keep warm. Prepare sauce while fish is cooking.

For sauce:

1. In a medium saucepan over medium-high heat, melt butter. Cook shallots and garlic until soft, but not browned. Add white wine and Pernod. Cook about 5 minutes or until reduced by about 1/4. Add chicken stock or broth and whipping cream, and again, cook until liquid is thick and reduced by about 1/4. Remove from heat and season with salt and pepper.

2. Remove fish from baking sheet and place on individual plates. Spoon about 1-2 tablespoons (15-30 mL) sauce over each portion and garnish with parsley or cilantro.

Serves: 6

COD WITH FRAGRANT VEGETABLES AND TOASTED ALMONDS

Cod, once a very inexpensive and readily available fish, has become increasingly scarce and costly in recent years due to over-fishing in the North Atlantic and Pacific oceans. This dish is worth investing in some tasty cod fillets.

1/4 cup (60 mL) butter

1 medium leek, white part only, cut into 2 inch (5 cm) lengths and sliced crosswise very thinly

1 large carrot, finely diced

Salt and freshly ground white pepper

2 pounds (1 kg) cod fillets (2-3 fillets work best-try to get them all close to the same size so they cook evenly)

1 cup (250 mL) finely diced onion

1 tablespoon (15 mL) finely diced jalapeno pepper

1 cup (250 mL) toasted sliced almonds

1/3 cup (75 mL) fresh lime juice

Salt and freshly ground white pepper

Fresh cilantro leaves for garnish

1. Preheat oven to 400°F (200°C). Lightly grease a large, rimmed baking sheet or casserole dish large enough to fit the cod fillets. Set aside.

2. In a medium saucepan, melt 2 tablespoons (30 mL) butter over medium high heat. Add leeks and sauté for 2 minutes. Add carrots and sauté an additional 5 minutes. Spread evenly on bottom of prepared baking sheet. Season with salt and white pepper to taste.

3. Return saucepan to heat and melt the remaining 2 tablespoons (30 mL) butter. Sauté onion and jalapeno until soft, about 5-7 minutes. Remove from heat and stir in almonds and lime juice. Season with salt and pepper.

4. Arrange fish over carrot/leek mixture. Spoon onion/almond mixture over fish. Bake in preheated oven 15-20 minutes or until thoroughly cooked. Fish is done when it flakes in the centre. Season with salt and white pepper and garnish with cilantro.

Serves: 6-8

CURRIED COCONUT MUSSELS

This is a delightfully simple and tasty dish. Using a commercial curry product saves you loads of time and gives wonderful flavour. You can use regular or light coconut milk, depending on your preference.

1 tablespoon (15 mL) vegetable oil

1/4 cup (60 mL) commercially prepared hot curry paste, such as Madras

2, 14-ounce (398 mL) cans coconut milk, regular or lite

1/2 cup (125 mL) fish or chicken broth or water

5 pounds (2.5 kg) fresh and well scrubbed mussels (discard any mussels that are open and do not close when lightly tapped)

1. In a large stock pot over medium heat, heat the vegetable oil and curry paste until smooth.

2. Add the coconut milk and broth or water and bring to a boil.

3. Add the mussels to the pot, cover and steam until all mussels are open. (Discard any mussels that do not open.)

4. Remove from heat and serve accompanied with sourdough or naan bread (Indian flatbread now available in most grocery stores) to mop up the curry sauce.

Serves: 4-6 as a first course

GREEK SHRIMP WITH TOMATO SAUCE AND FETA

This simple shrimp dish gets its flavour from a well-seasoned tomato sauce and from the feta cheese and fresh basil added at the end of cooking. Shrimp come in all sizes ranging anywhere from 10-100 shrimp per pound (500 g). They are often sold frozen according to size – for example, extra-large shrimp are size 16-20, meaning that you get 16-20 shrimp per pound (500 g), whereas miniature shrimp are size 100, meaning you get 100 per pound (500 g). For this dish, I like the shrimp to take centre stage, so I like to buy a larger shrimp, about size 16-20. The key to a tasty shrimp is to cook it just until it's pink throughout – overcooking shrimp turns them very tough and rubbery.

2 tablespoons (30 mL) extra virgin olive oil

2 tablespoons (30 mL) butter

1/2 cup (125 mL) finely chopped onion

4 garlic cloves, finely minced

19-ounce (540 mL) can plum tomatoes, drained and juice discarded

1/2 cup (125 mL) dry white wine

1/4 cup (60 mL) finely chopped fresh parsley

2 teaspoons (10 mL) dried oregano

1 teaspoon (5 mL) dried basil

1/2 teaspoon (2.5 mL) dried red chilli flakes (optional)

1 teaspoon (5 mL) salt

Freshly ground black pepper

2 pounds (1 kg) raw shrimp, peeled and de-veined

4 ounces (120 g) feta cheese, cut into 1/4 inch (0.5 cm) cubes

1/4 cup (125 mL) chopped fresh basil

1. In a large saucepan, add oil and melt butter over medium-high heat. Sauté onion until soft, but not browned, about 5 minutes. Add garlic and cook one more minute. Add tomatoes, wine, parsley, oregano, basil, chilli flakes (if using), salt, and pepper.

2. Bring to a boil and then reduce heat to low. Simmer, uncovered, for 30-45 minutes, stirring occasionally, until thick.

3. Add shrimp and feta cheese to sauce. Cook until shrimp turns pink and feta begins to slightly melt (about 8-10 minutes). Garnish with fresh basil.

4. Serve atop a bed of cooked rice or orzo pasta.

Makes: 8 first course or 4 entrée servings

HONEYED CHICKEN BREASTS WITH TARRAGON SOUR CREAM

The flavours in this dish are fresh and the sauce is silky smooth. Serve this with a brown rice and mushroom pilaf and a mixture of steamed carrots and green beans with chopped fresh herbs.

4 boneless, skinless chicken breasts
[1- 1/2 pounds (500-750 g)]

Salt and freshly ground pepper

1-2 tablespoons (15-30 mL) olive oil

3/4 cup (175 mL) chicken broth

3/4 cup (175 mL) sour cream, regular or fat-reduced

2 tablespoons (30 mL) Dijon mustard

2 tablespoons (30 mL) honey

1 teaspoon (5 mL) dried tarragon leaves

1. Wash chicken breasts and pat dry. Season with salt and freshly ground black pepper.

2. Heat a 10 inch (25 cm) skillet to medium high. Add oil and swirl to coat the pan. Add chicken breasts (be sure they 'sizzle' so you know the pan is hot enough); reduce heat to medium, and cook for 8-10 minutes or until bottom is golden brown. Turn breasts over and cook an additional 8 minutes. Remove to a clean warm plate.

3. In the same skillet, increase heat to high. Deglaze the pan with the chicken broth, being sure to scrape up the brown bits. Cook for 1-2 minutes to reduce slightly. Add sour cream, mustard, honey, and tarragon, and stir to combine. Bring to a low boil and return the chicken breasts to the pan, spooning sauce over the chicken. Cook an additional 8-10 minutes or until chicken is no longer pink inside. Remove from pan and serve.

Serves: 4

GRILLED SHRIMP SALAD WITH SPICY PEANUT DRESSING

I first served this dish for a ladies luncheon and got rave reviews! The dressing is similar to a satay sauce, just thinned down to a pouring consistency. You can change the salad by varying the vegetable toppings such as using snow peas and cucumber or left-over steamed broccoli or cauliflower. Grilled flank steak or pork tenderloin medallions also work well as a substitute for shrimp if you prefer. Mirin is a very low alcohol wine made from rice. Samal Oelek® is mixture of chillies and spices and is widely used throughout Indonesia, Malaysia, and southern India. It should be readily available in most grocery stores.

Salad:

4 cups (1 L) Mesclun mix salad

4 cups (1 L) baby spinach

3 green onions, green part only,
sliced in 1 inch (2.5 cm) pieces on the diagonal

1 red pepper, cored and de-veined, sliced into thin strips

12 trimmed asparagus spears, blanched, chilled,
and cut into 2 inch (5 cm) lengths

Shrimp:

1 1/2 pounds (750 g) raw shrimp, peeled, and de-veined,
16-20 per pound (500 g)

1 tablespoon (15 mL) vegetable oil

2 teaspoons (10 mL) commercially prepared
Cajun seasoning

Dressing:

2/3 cup (150 mL) creamy peanut butter

2 garlic cloves, finely minced

2 tablespoons (30 mL) honey

2 tablespoons (30 mL) mirin

1/3 cup (75 mL) soy sauce

1/2 cup (125 mL) rice wine vinegar

1 teaspoon (5 mL) grated fresh ginger root

1 teaspoon (5 mL) Sambal Oelek®

1/4 cup (60 mL) water

2 tablespoons (30 mL) toasted sesame seeds

Continued...

GRILLED SHRIMP SALAD WITH SPICY PEANUT DRESSING

continued...

Mesclun is a popular mixture of baby salad greens. Common greens in Mesclun mix include dandelion greens, arugula, oak leaf, mache, and several others. If you can't find Mesclun mix, use chopped Romaine lettuce or all baby spinach.

For salad:

Combine lettuce, spinach, onions, peppers, and asparagus in a large bowl and set aside.

For shrimp:

In a small bowl, toss shrimp with Cajun seasoning to coat. Heat a large skillet to medium high and add oil. Add shrimp and cook 2-3 minutes on each side just until they turn pink, but not overcooked. Remove from pan and set aside.

For dressing:

Combine all ingredients in a blender or food processor. Season with salt and pepper to taste; refrigerate until use.

Assembly:

Toss salad with half the dressing (pass the remaining dressing around the table); place about 1 1/2 cups (375 mL) of salad on each plate; top with 4-5 shrimp each; garnish with sesame seeds.

Serves: 6

PANKO CRUSTED HALIBUT WITH GINGER AND SESAME SEEDS

Panko is a style of breadcrumbs used in Japanese cooking. The crumbs are substantially larger and crispier than traditional North American breadcrumbs, and they add delightful crunch to this dish. Sesame seeds come in shades of white, red, brown, and black; by far, the white sesame seed is the most popular. If you have difficulty finding the black, you can use all white sesame seeds.

2 inch (5 cm) piece of fresh ginger, peeled and sliced into thin strips

4 green onions, white part only, sliced into 2 inch (5 cm) pieces

1/4 cup (60 mL) vegetable oil

4 halibut steaks [1-1/2 pounds (500-750 g)]

Salt and freshly ground white pepper

1/4 cup (60 mL) EACH white and black sesame seeds (use all white if you can't find black)

3/4 cup (175 mL) panko bread crumbs

1. In a small saucepan, warm oil, but do not overheat. Remove from heat and stir in ginger and green onions. Set aside for one hour to let flavours infuse and then refrigerate until completely cool. Be sure the infused oil is completely cool before proceeding.

2. In a re-sealable plastic bag, place infused oil and halibut steaks. Marinate for 2-4 hours in the refrigerator.

3. When ready to prepare, preheat oven to 375°F (190°C). Remove steaks from marinade and place on clean dry plate. Discard marinade. Season halibut steaks with salt and white pepper.

4. In a small bowl, combine sesame seeds and panko crumbs. Coat each side of halibut steaks with crumb mixture. Heat a non-stick skillet to medium high heat; place fish in skillet and brown on one side, about 3-4 minutes. Transfer halibut steaks to baking sheet, browned side up. Finish cooking in preheated 375°F (190°C) oven for about 15 minutes until fish flesh flakes when a fork is inserted and slightly twisted (cooking time will vary depending on the thickness of the fish).

5. Remove from oven when cooked.

Serves: 4

SPICY COCONUT CHICKEN

Boneless, skinless chicken thighs are a nice alternative to chicken breast. The dark meat of the chicken holds up well to the flavours in this dish and they are the perfect portion size for small appetites.

2 pounds (1 kg) boneless, skinless chicken thighs

3 tablespoons (30 mL) vegetable oil

1 medium onion, finely diced

1 teaspoon (5 mL) EACH ground coriander, cumin, and salt

1 tablespoon (15 mL) freshly grated, peeled ginger root

1 tablespoon (15 mL) hot chilli sauce, such as Sambal Oelek®

2 tablespoons (30 mL) crunchy peanut butter

2 tablespoons (30 mL) soy sauce

14-ounce (398 mL) can coconut milk, regular or lite

2 teaspoons (10 mL) finely grated lime zest

1. In a large skillet, heat 1 tablespoon (15 mL) vegetable oil and brown half the chicken on all sides. Remove and set aside on a clean plate. Repeat with remainder of chicken.

2. Heat remaining 1 tablespoon (15 mL) vegetable oil and add onion, coriander, cumin, salt, and ginger root. Sauté until onion is soft. Add hot chilli sauce, peanut butter and soy sauce and blend well. Add coconut milk and browned chicken to skillet. Cover and cook 20-30 minutes until chicken is cooked through. Remove to serving dish and garnish with lime zest.

3. Serve with steamed basmati rice.

Serves: 6

JUST A 'BIT O' BUTTER' CHICKEN

Butter chicken is a dish of Indian descent known for its buttery flavour and creamy sauce. Here, all of the flavour comes through, but without excessive fat by using mostly 2% milk and just a small amount of cereal cream. Don't be turned off by the number of ingredients; chances are good that you have most of them in your pantry.

Chicken and Marinade:

2 pounds (1 kg) boneless skinless chicken breast, cut into 2 inch (5 cm) pieces

1/2 teaspoon (2.5 mL) ground turmeric

1 teaspoon (5 mL) ground cayenne pepper

1 teaspoon (5 mL) ground paprika

1 teaspoon (5 mL) ground coriander

1 1/2 teaspoons (7.5 mL) ground cumin

2 tablespoons (30 mL) vegetable oil

Pinch of salt and pepper

2 teaspoons (10 mL) minced fresh ginger root

2 teaspoons (10 mL) minced garlic

Sauce:

2 tablespoons (30 mL) butter

2 tablespoons (30 mL) all-purpose flour

1/2 teaspoon (2.5 mL) salt

1 teaspoon (5 mL) cayenne pepper

1 cup (250 mL) canned crushed tomatoes

2 cups (500 mL) 2% milk

1/2 cup (125 mL) cereal cream

White granulated sugar (if needed, to reduce acidic taste)

Continued...

JUST A 'BIT O' BUTTER' CHICKEN
continued...

For chicken:

1. Combine all marinade ingredients in a re-sealable plastic bag. Be sure all chicken pieces are well coated with marinade. Marinate for at least 1 hour or up to 8 hours in the refrigerator.

2. Preheat oven to 350°F (180°C).

3. After chicken has marinated, remove from marinade and transfer to baking sheet lined with parchment paper; discard marinade. Bake in preheated oven for 20 minutes or until thoroughly cooked.

For sauce:

1. In a medium saucepan over medium-high heat, melt butter and add flour. Stir constantly for 1-2 minutes. Add salt, cayenne pepper, and tomatoes, and stir well. Add milk and stir until mixture begins to thicken. Bring to a low boil. Immediately reduce heat and simmer for 10-15 minutes until mixture thickens more. Add cream and stir to form a smooth sauce. Do not allow the sauce to fully boil or it may separate.

2. Taste sauce. If the flavour is quite acidic, begin to add white granulated sugar in 1 tablespoon (15 mL) increments until acidity is reduced.

3. Add cooked chicken to sauce. Bring to a simmer once again and cook for 10 minutes to ensure flavours blend. Serve with steamed basmati rice.

Serves: 4

SALMON WITH FOUR MARINADES

Here are 4 simple and tasty marinades for salmon. Salmon is a fatty fish, rich in omega-3 fatty acids (the good kind for heart health). I simply love the marriage of maple and salmon, so it's no surprise that 3 of these marinades contain maple syrup! Be sure to use real maple syrup and not imitation. Once marinated, be sure to discard the marinade and do not reuse.

ASIAN MARINADE WITH LEMONGRASS

1/2 cup (125 mL) rice wine vinegar

1/3 cup (75 mL) sesame oil

1/2 cup (125 mL) maple syrup

3 garlic cloves, minced

1 tablespoon (15 mL) finely minced ginger root

3/4 cup (175 mL) soy sauce

1/2 cup (125 mL) coarsely chopped stalks of lemon grass

1. In a medium glass or ceramic bowl, combine all ingredients to create marinade.
2. Marinate 1 1/2 pounds (750 g) of salmon side or four 4-6 (120g-180 g) ounce salmon steaks for 8-12 hours. Be sure to remove lemon grass before cooking.
3. Bake in a preheated 400°F (200°C) oven or grill until cooked. A general rule of thumb is to cook 10 minutes for every 1 inch (2.5 cm) thickness of salmon.

BOURBON MARINADE

1/2 cup(125 mL) bourbon whisky

3/4 cup (175 mL) soy sauce

1/2 cup (125 mL) maple syrup

1/4 cup (60 mL) brown sugar

1 tablespoon (15 mL) finely minced ginger root

2 garlic cloves, finely minced

1. In a medium glass or ceramic bowl, combine all ingredients to create marinade.
2. Marinate 1 1/2 pounds (750 g) of salmon side or four 4-6 (120-180 g) ounce salmon steaks for 8-12 hours. Drain marinade before cooking.
3. Bake in a preheated 400°F (200°C) oven or grill until cooked. A general rule of thumb is to cook 10 minutes for every 1 inch (2.5 cm) thickness of salmon.

SALMON WITH FOUR MARINADES
continued...

SIMPLE SIMON MAPLE MARINADE

1 cup (250 mL) maple syrup

1 cup (250 mL) soy sauce

4 garlic cloves, finely minced

1 tablespoon (15 mL) finely grated fresh ginger root

1. In a medium glass or ceramic bowl, combine all ingredients to create marinade.

2. Marinate 1 1/2 pounds (750 g) of salmon side or four 4-6 (120g-180 g) ounce salmon steaks for 8-12 hours. Drain marinade before cooking.

3. Bake in a preheated 400°F (200°C) oven or grill until cooked. A general rule of thumb is to cook 10 minutes for every 1 inch (2.5 cm) thickness of salmon.

SCOTCH SALMON

1/2 cup (125 mL) freshly squeezed orange juice

Grated zest of 1 orange

1/3 cup (75 mL) Scotch whisky
(choose one according to your taste preference)

1 tablespoon (15 mL) honey

1 tablespoon (15 mL) Dijon mustard

2 teaspoons (10 mL) Worcestershire sauce

1. In a medium glass or ceramic bowl, combine all ingredients.

2. Marinate 1 1/2 pounds (750 g) of salmon side or four 4-6ounce (120-180 g) salmon steaks for 8-12 hours.

3. Bake in a preheated 400°F (200°C) oven or grill until cooked. A general rule of thumb is to cook 10 minutes for every 1 inch (2.5 cm) thickness of salmon.

PAN ROASTED COD WITH GINGER, MISO, AND CILANTRO

Miso is one of the key elements in Japanese cooking. It is a bean paste made from soybeans, available in colours ranging from yellow to red to dark brown, each with its own unique flavour. The one recommended here is the all-purpose yellow variety. If you can't find miso, you can substitute soy sauce, but the flavour of the sauce won't be quite as rich or intense.

Cod:

1 1/2 pounds (750 g) cod fillet; remove as many bones as you can

Salt and pepper to taste

About 1/2 cup (125 mL) all-purpose flour, for coating

2 tablespoons (30 mL) vegetable oil

Sauce:

2 teaspoons (10 mL) sesame oil

1/3 cup (75 mL) finely diced shallots

2 teaspoons (10 mL) finely minced fresh ginger root

1/4 cup (60 mL) fresh orange juice

1 cup (250 mL) chicken stock or broth

1 tablespoon (15 mL) rice vinegar

2 tablespoons (30 mL) yellow miso (or soy sauce if unavailable)

2 tablespoons (30 mL) chopped fresh cilantro

Continued...

PAN ROASTED COD WITH GINGER, MISO, AND CILANTRO

continued...

For cod:

1. Preheat oven to 400°F (200°C).

2. Season both sides of cod with salt and pepper. Coat with flour and shake off excess.

3. Heat 1 tablespoon (15 mL) vegetable oil in a saucepan until hot, but not smoking. Brown cod fillets, one at at time, on one side. When browned, remove to a plate and blot with paper towel to remove any excess fat. Transfer partially cooked fish to parchment-lined baking sheet, brown side up. Repeat with remaining fillets until all are partially cooked.

4. Place fillets in preheated oven and bake until fully cooked, about 10 minutes depending on thickness of fish. Remove from oven and top each fillet with about 2 tablespoons (30 mL) sauce and serve.

For sauce:

1. In a medium saucepan, heat sesame oil over medium heat. Add shallots and ginger and cook until soft about 3 minutes; do not brown.

2. Add orange juice, broth, and vinegar. Bring to a boil and then reduce heat so that sauce simmers. Simmer until reduced to about 2/3 cup (150 mL) in total.

3. Stir in miso and cilantro and simmer for 1 more minute.

Serves: 6

ROAST CHICKEN STUFFED WITH AUTUMN FRUITS

So, aren't all chickens created equal? No, not really, as there are several classifications of chicken, each suited to different cooking methods. Here's a simple lesson: Broiler-fryers are the youngest chickens (2-3 months old) and hence weigh the least (up to about 3 1/2 pounds [1.75kg]). They are lower in fat than others and best suited to being broiled, grilled, or fried. Roasters are a little older (up to 8 months), weigh a bit more (up to 5 pounds [2.5kg]), have a bit more fat, and are best suited to roasting methods. The oldest (up to 18 months) and heaviest (up to 6 pounds [3kg]) chickens, sometimes called hens, are stewing chickens. Their meat is tougher and benefits from a longer cooking time and moist cooking method, such as braising or stewing, to help tenderize the meat.

1 large roaster chicken, about 3-4 pounds (1.5-2 kg)

Stuffing:

1 cup (250 mL) mixed dried fruits of your choice, such as dried apricots, raisins, prunes, cranberries, cherries, or other (equal parts apricots and cranberries is my favourite)

1/4 cup (125 mL) dry white wine or dry sherry

1 tablespoon (15 mL) butter

4 strips bacon, diced

1/2 cup (125 mL) finely diced onions

1/2 cup (125 mL) finely diced celery

6 slices (about 4 cups [1 L]), day old white or whole wheat bread, crusts removed, and cut into 1/2 inch (1 cm) cubes

1 large egg

1/4 cup (60 mL) chopped fresh parsley

1/4 cup (60 mL) chicken stock or broth or water, approximately (if needed)

1. Rinse the chicken well and pat dry. Season outside of bird with salt and pepper and set aside.

For stuffing:

1. In a small mixing bowl, combine dried fruit with white wine and let soak for 30 minutes. Drain fruit and set aside; reserve wine marinade.

2. Preheat oven to 375°F (190°C).

3. In a large skillet over medium-high heat, melt butter and sauté bacon, onions, and celery until onions are soft and bacon is semi-crisp but not brown. Remove from heat. Transfer mixture to a large mixing bowl and let cool slightly, about 10 minutes.

Continued...

ROAST CHICKEN STUFFED WITH AUTUMN FRUITS
continued...

4. Add bread cubes and egg. Stir to combine. Stir in the wine-marinated dried fruit and parsley. Moisten first with the drained wine marinade and then with chicken stock or water if necessary so that the stuffing holds together.

5. Stuff the cavity of the chicken loosely with the stuffing. If there is excess stuffing, place it in a small buttered casserole dish and bake separately in the oven until heated through.

6. Cook chicken until internal temperature registers 175°F (79°C), about 1 1/2-2 hours. Let rest about 15 minutes under an aluminum foil tent.

6. Remove stuffing from cavity and carve chicken.

Serve this chicken to your family or dinner guests with Glazed Beets with Balsamic Vinegar and Rosemary (page 153). Finish the meal with Christine's Self-Saucing Lemon Pudding (page 188).

Serves: 6

CAVATELLI WITH BROCCOLI AND MUSHROOMS

There are literally hundreds of shapes of pasta. Shapes add not only variety, but can have an effect on the overall quality of the finished dish. Generally speaking, shaped pastas such as cavatappi (corkscrews), fusilli (little springs), or penne (quills) pair best with sauces that have texture. Bits and pieces of meat, beans, or vegetables can nestle into the nooks and crannies of the shapes. Long, thin pastas, such as capellini (angel hair) and spaghetti (little strings) marry best with olive oil or light cream sauces, while long, thick pastas such as linguine (little tongues) or fettuccine (little ribbons) can carry a thick cream or tomato-based sauce.

My mother used to make the cavatelli (shell-shaped pasta with short, narrow, rippled edges) from scratch which made this dish divine, but here, dried pasta will work just fine.

1 pound (500 g) dried cavatelli noodles (or penne or fusilli)

2 cups (500 mL) fresh broccoli tops, cut into very small florets

2 cups (500 mL) fresh thinly sliced white mushrooms

1/4 cup (60 mL) butter

4 garlic cloves, finely minced

1 cup (250 mL) part-skim or regular fat mozzarella cheese

Freshly ground black pepper

1. Preheat oven to 350°F (180°C).
2. Cook pasta in boiling, salted water until al dente. Drain and place in large, lightly buttered oven proof casserole dish.
3. Blanch broccoli in boiling water until bright green and only slightly tender. Refresh under cold water to stop cooking. Drain and add to casserole dish.
4. In a medium skillet, melt butter. Add mushrooms and cook until water is released and they begin to wilt. Add garlic and cook 2-4 minutes longer. Add to casserole dish.
5. Mix ingredients in casserole dish gently. Sprinkle with mozzarella cheese and freshly ground black pepper. Cover and bake for 30 minutes or until cheese is melted.

Serves: 6-8, depending on if it's used as a first course or main dish

LINGUINE WITH RED CLAM SAUCE

When cooking with wine, a general rule of thumb is to only use wine that you're prepared to drink!

2 tablespoons (30 mL) olive oil

2 tablespoons (30 mL) butter

1 cup (250 mL) finely chopped onion

12 garlic cloves, finely minced

6 ounces (180 mL) dry white wine

1/2 cup (125 mL) chicken stock or broth

1 1/2 cups (375 mL) canned whole plum tomatoes, drained, and juice discarded

2 tablespoons (30 mL) finely chopped fresh parsley

1 teaspoon (5 mL) dried oregano

1 teaspoon (5 mL) dried basil

1/2 teaspoon (2.5 mL) chilli pepper flakes

2, 10-ounce (284 mL) cans baby clams, not drained

1 pound (500 g) dry linguine

Freshly ground black pepper

1. In a large shallow saucepan on medium heat, heat olive oil and butter. Sweat onion until soft. Add garlic and sauté 1-2 minutes more, being careful not to burn.

2. Add wine, chicken broth, tomatoes, parsley, oregano, basil, and chilli flakes. Bring to a boil. Reduce heat and simmer for 30 minutes. Add clams and clam juice and simmer for 10 additional minutes.

3. Cook pasta in boiling, salted water until al dente. Drain. Cover with sauce, top with freshly ground black pepper, and serve.

Serves: 8-10

BAKED PENNE WITH CHEESE AND OLIVES

Penne is large, straight tubes of pasta cut on the diagonal. I've made this dish with other types of pasta such as rotini (spirals), bow-ties, and elbows with great success. You can also use whole wheat pasta for added fibre and a slightly nutty flavour.

For Tomato Sauce:

1/4 cup (60 mL) olive oil

1 1/2 cups (375 mL) finely chopped white or yellow onions

4 garlic cloves, finely minced

2, 28-ounce (796 mL) cans plum tomatoes, drained, coarsely chopped and juice discarded

1 tablespoon (15 mL) dried basil

1 tablespoon (15 mL) dried oregano

5 1/2-ounce (156 mL) can tomato paste

1 1/2 teaspoons (7.5 mL) dried red pepper flakes (optional)

1 cup (250 mL) chicken stock or broth

1 tablespoon sugar (15 mL) (or more) to taste

1. In a large sauce pot, heat oil and sauté onions until transparent, about 5 minutes. Add garlic and sauté an additional 2 minutes.

2. Add remaining ingredients and bring to a boil. Reduce heat so that mixture simmers. Cover and simmer for 1 – 1 1/2 hours, stirring occasionally. Taste and adjust seasoning with salt, pepper, and sugar (as needed).

Makes: 6 cups (1.5 L)

Continued...

BAKED PENNE WITH CHEESE AND OLIVES
continued...

For Pasta:

1 pound (500 g) dry penne pasta

1 cup (250 mL) shredded part-skim mozzarella cheese

1 cup (250 mL) shredded Havarti cheese

1/2 cup (125 mL) drained and pitted Kalamata olives, coarsely chopped

1/2 cup (125 mL) grated Parmesan cheese

Freshly ground black pepper

1. Preheat oven to 375°F (190°C). Lightly grease a 9x13 inch (3 L) casserole dish.

2. In a large pot of boiling salted water, cook penne until al dente. Remove from heat, drain and pour into large mixing bowl. Pour sauce over pasta and stir to combine. Stir in mozzarella and Havarti cheeses.

3. Transfer mixture to prepared dish. Sprinkle with olives and Parmesan cheese. Cover loosely with aluminum foil and bake in preheated 375°F (190°C) oven for 30 minutes or until cheese is melted and mixture is heated through. Finish with a generous grinding of black pepper.

Serves: 8-10

HOMEMADE MANICOTTI WITH THREE CHEESES

When I was young, this dish was often served at special family dinners. To make the job easier, we often made the shells and filling the day before, covered and refrigerated them separately overnight, and then assembled the next day. This dish is truly worth the effort and one that could benefit from the help of a partner.

Manicotti Shells:

2 cups (500 mL) all-purpose flour

1 teaspoon (5 mL) salt

2 1/2 cups (625 mL) water

4 large eggs

1. In a large mixing bowl, combine flour and salt.
2. In a small bowl, combine water and eggs and whisk well. Pour egg mixture into flour mixture and mix well with a wooden spoon until smooth and no lumps remain.
3. Heat 5 inch (13 cm) non-stick skillet over medium high heat. Pour in 1/3 cup (75 mL) of mixture and swirl to coat pan. Cook for 1-2 minutes until small bubbles form. Carefully turn over with a small spatula and cook for 1 more minute. Remove from heat and begin to stack shells, being sure to separate shells with parchment or waxed paper.
4. Continue until 22-24 shells are made.

Continued...

HOMEMADE MANICOTTI WITH THREE CHEESES
continued...

Cheese Filling:

1 pound (500 g) ricotta cheese

1/2 pound (250 g) shredded mozzarella cheese, part-skim or regular fat

1 cup (250 mL) grated Parmesan cheese

3 large eggs, beaten well

1/2 cup (125 mL) finely chopped fresh parsley

1/2 teaspoon (2.5 mL) salt

1 teaspoon (5 mL) freshly ground black pepper

1. Preheat oven to 350°F (180°C).

2. In a large mixing bowl, combine all ingredients and mix lightly with a wooden spoon. Do not use a mixer or mixture will be too thin.

3. Place 1 manicotti shell on a clean work surface. Place 1/3 cup (75 mL) filling down the centre of the shell. Fold ends over. Place manicotti seam side down in lightly greased 9x13 inch (3 L) baking dish. Continue to roll until pan is full, leaving about 1/4 inch (0.5 cm) between each shell.

4. When pan is full, top with your favourite tomato sauce and bake for 25 minutes or until heated through completely. Sprinkle with extra grated Parmesan cheese and serve.

Serves: 6-8

LINGUINE MARGARITA

The colour in this dish resembles the colours of the Italian flag: red, white, and green! It's called Margarita because when a chef first made a pizza for Italy's Princess Margarita long ago, he used red (tomato sauce), white (cheese), and green (basil).

This pasta is full of flavour. Add a tossed green salad and you have a delightful everyday meal. I find it best to start boiling the water for the pasta at the same time as you start to cook the sauce – this way, both components will be hot when you need them.

2 tablespoons (30 mL) olive oil

1/4 cup (60 mL) finely diced onion

1 pound (500 g) fresh asparagus, tough ends discarded, trimmed and cut into 2 inch (5 cm) lengths

3 garlic cloves, finely minced

1 cup (250 mL) drained, patted dry, and coarsely chopped, oil packed sun-dried tomatoes,

3/4 cup (175 mL) dry white wine

1/4 cup (60 mL) cereal or whipping cream

3/4 pound (375 g) dry linguine pasta

1/2 cup (125 mL) grated Parmesan cheese

1/4 cup (60 mL) chopped fresh basil

1. In a large skillet, heat oil over medium-high heat. Add onion and asparagus and cook until asparagus is slightly soft and bright green, about 3 minutes. Add garlic and sauté 1-2 minutes until fragrant, being careful not to burn garlic. Remove with a slotted spoon to a plate and keep warm.

2. To the same skillet, add tomatoes and white wine. Cover and simmer over low heat until the tomatoes are softened, about 8-10 minutes. Return asparagus to skillet and add cream. Cook 2-3 minutes to meld flavours. Season to taste with salt and pepper.

3. In a large pot, bring salted water to a boil. Add pasta and cook until al dente. Strain and place in a serving bowl. Cover with sauce and stir to combine. Top with Parmesan cheese, garnish with fresh basil, and serve.

Serves: 4

RIGATONI WITH ITALIAN SAUSAGE AND COLOURFUL PEPPERS

Cooking pasta to the 'al dente' stage means cooking 'to the tooth'. The pasta is cooked until it is slightly chewy and some of the starch sticks to the tooth. My mother-in-law used to throw a piece of pasta at the refrigerator – if it stuck, it was done. I prefer a cleaner approach: simply remove a piece and taste it! Rigatoni (grooved tubes of macaroni) can take up to 15-20 minutes to cook, so I like to start cooking the pasta and sausage at the same time.

2 pounds (1 kg) hot or mild Italian sausage, cut into 1 inch (2.5 cm) pieces

1/4 cup (60 mL) olive oil

4 garlic cloves, finely minced

1 teaspoon (5 mL) chilli flakes (or more to taste)

2 medium red bell peppers, cored, seeded, and cut into 1/2 inch (1 cm) strips

2 medium yellow bell peppers, cored, seeded, and cut into 1/2 inch (1 cm) strips

1 pound (500 g) dry rigatoni pasta

2 tablespoons (30 mL) butter

1 cup (250 mL) freshly grated Parmesan cheese

1/4 cup (60 mL) EACH finely chopped fresh parsley and fresh basil

Freshly ground black pepper, to taste

1. Fill a large skillet with 1 inch (2.5 cm) of water. Bring to a boil and cook sausage pieces for 10-12 minutes. Drain water and brown sausage in the same skillet (about 5-7 minutes). Remove sausage from the pan and keep warm.

2. In the same skillet, heat olive oil over medium heat. Add peppers and cook until skins brown but the peppers do not go limp. Add garlic and chilli flakes and cook 1-2 minutes more. Add reserved sausage to pepper mixture and cook an additional 5 minutes.

3. In a separate pot, cook rigatoni in salted boiling water until al dente. Drain and place in a large serving dish. Add butter and stir to coat.

4. Add sausage/pepper mixture to rigatoni and stir well. Garnish with Parmesan cheese, parsley, basil, and freshly ground black pepper.

Serves: 8

SPINACH, BASIL, AND RICOTTA GNOCCHI WITH MUSHROOMS AND PINE NUTS

Pronounced 'nee-oh-kee', gnocchi are Italy's version of dumplings. They are traditionally made using mashed potatoes, but here, a lighter version is made using ricotta cheese and spinach. This dough is quite wet, so be patient.

Gnocchi:

2/3 cup (150 mL) cooked spinach, from fresh or frozen spinach, water completely squeezed out and finely chopped

1/4 cup (60 mL) chopped fresh basil

1 1/2 cups (375 mL) ricotta cheese

2 large egg yolks

1/2 teaspoon (2.5 mL) salt

1/4 teaspoon (1.25 mL) ground nutmeg

2 garlic cloves, finely minced

1/2 cup (125 mL) all-purpose flour, plus more for dusting

Sauce:

1/4 cup (60 mL) butter

1/2 cup (125 mL) finely sliced white button mushrooms

1/4 cup (60 mL) fruity dry white wine

1/4 cup (60 mL) Parmesan cheese, finely grated

1/4 cup (60 mL) pine nuts, lightly toasted

For Gnocchi:

1. In a medium mixing bowl, combine spinach, basil, ricotta cheese, egg yolks, salt, garlic, nutmeg, and flour. Stir to form a soft dough.

2. Cut dough into 4 pieces. Dust lightly with flour. You want to use enough flour to keep them from sticking, but not so much that they become excessively 'doughy'.

Continued...

Rigatoni with Italian Sausage and Colourful Peppers
page 121

Muffaletta
page 128

SPINACH, BASIL, AND RICOTTA GNOCCHI WITH MUSHROOMS AND PINE NUTS
continued...

3. On a generously floured work surface, gently roll each piece into a long rope, 3/4 inches (1.5 cm) thick and about 15 inches (38 cm) long.

4. Cut each rope into 1 inch (2.5 cm) long pieces to form gnocchi.

5. In two batches, drop gnocchi into boiling, salted water. They will immediately sink to the bottom and then rise to the top after about a minute. Reduce the heat to a low boil (if water boils too hard, the gnocchi will break) and cook for 2-3 minutes until tender. Remove to a lightly oiled plate and keep separated to prevent sticking. Repeat until all gnocchi are blanched.

For sauce:

Heat butter in a large skillet; add mushrooms and sauté for 1-2 minutes but do not brown. Add gnocchi and sauté lightly for 2-3 minutes, being sure to keep them separated. Add the wine and reduce until most of the wine is evaporated. Remove to individual serving plates and garnish with Parmesan cheese and toasted pine nuts. Season with freshly ground black pepper if desired.

Serves: 6-8 as a first course

SPAGHETTINI CARBONARA

This dish has only a few simple ingredients, but the flavour is amazing. The sauce can become quite thick, so it's best served as soon as it's ready. Complement this rich dish with a fresh, crisp salad.

1/2 pound (250 g) sliced bacon
1/2 cup (125 mL) whipping cream
1/2 cup (125 mL) homogenized milk
4 large egg yolks
1/2 cup (125 mL) grated Parmesan cheese
1 pound (500 g) spaghettini, cooked to al-dente
1-2 teaspoons (5-10 mL) freshly ground black pepper

1. In a large skillet, cook bacon until medium crisp. Drain fat and discard. Crumble bacon into small pieces.

2. In a small mixing bowl, whisk cream, milk, and egg yolks until smooth. Transfer to a simmering double boiler. Stir mixture constantly until it begins to thicken enough to coat the back of a spoon. Be sure to stir constantly so you don't end up with scrambled eggs! When mixture is thick, remove from heat and add Parmesan cheese and reserved bacon. Spoon hot sauce over hot spaghettini that has been cooked to 'al dente', drained and placed in a large serving bowl.

3. Garnish with freshly ground black pepper. This sounds like a lot of black pepper, but the sharp taste of the pepper really complements the rich sauce.

Serves: 4-6

OPEN-FACED SANDWICH WITH AVOCADO, TOMATO, PROSCIUTTO, AND BASIL

What a lovely mix of textures and flavours in this open-faced sandwich. While botanically a fruit, avocados have an unusually high fat content, so calorie-conscious folks often avoid them. Thankfully, the fat is mostly mono-unsaturated, the healthier type of fat. Avocados also provide dietary fibre and a host of other vitamins and minerals. Used in moderation, this delightful fruit with a velvety smooth texture and buttery flavour is a nice addition to a balanced meal plan.

Avocados are ready to eat when they yield to gentle palm pressure. They ripen well at home by placing 2 or more touching each other in a loosely closed paper bag on the kitchen counter. Once ripened, they will hold for another 2-4 days in the refrigerator.

6 slices thick cut (3/4 inch [1.5 cm]) hearty multi-grain bread

Olive oil for basting

1 garlic clove, split in half

1/2 teaspoon (2.5 mL) dried oregano

3 medium plum tomatoes, stemmed and sliced 1/2 inch (1 cm) thick lengthwise

1 large avocado, peeled, halved, pitted, and sliced into 12 slices

6 paper thin slices (about 3 ounces [90g]) prosciutto

6 shaved slices Parmesan cheese

12 fresh basil leaves

Freshly ground black pepper

1. Preheat a large, non-stick skillet to medium heat.

2. Brush top and bottom of bread lightly with olive oil. Sprinkle with a few grains of dried oregano. Grill in skillet on each side for 30-60 seconds until lightly toasted. Remove from heat and rub with garlic clove.

3. On a serving plate, top each slice of bread with 2-3 tomato slices, 2 avocado slices, 1 prosciutto slice, 1 shaving of Parmesan cheese and 2 fresh basil leaves. Top with freshly ground black pepper.

Makes: 6 open-faced sandwiches

MUFFALETTA

Muffaletta is native to New Orleans, dating back to the early 1900s. This is a perfect picnic item. Make it the day before, then pack it with you (chilled), and slice and serve at a picnic lunch.

Mortadella is an Italian deli meat which originated in Bologna, Italy, and from which the popular lunch meat, 'baloney' originated. It also has added small cubes of pork fat – not exactly the best choice for those watching their energy intake. In fact, Muffaletta is a higher calorie choice, so keep your slices thin and savour the flavour of every bite. You can reduce the fat and calories in this dish by using lower fat meats such as turkey and lower fat cheese. The flavour will not be authentic, but the choice is yours.

Olive Salad:

1 1/2 cups (375 mL) EACH drained and pitted Kalamata and pimiento stuffed green olives

1/4 cup (60 mL) olive oil

4-ounce jar (113 mL) pimientos, drained

1/3 cup (75 mL) chopped fresh parsley

3 anchovies (optional), drained

1 tablespoon (15 mL) drained capers

1 tablespoon (15 mL) finely minced fresh garlic

1 tablespoon (15 mL) finely chopped fresh basil

1 teaspoon (5 mL) dried oregano

1/4 tsp (1.25 mL) salt

1/2 tsp (2.5 mL) freshly ground pepper

Muffaletta:

8 inch (20 cm) round loaf peasant style Italian bread

4 ounces (120 g) EACH thinly sliced Italian salami, mortadella, and provolone cheese

Continued...

MUFFALETTA
continued...

For olive salad:

1. In a food processor, combine olives, olive oil, pimientos, parsley, anchovies, capers, garlic, basil, oregano, salt, and pepper. Pulse a few times until finely chopped, but not pureed. Set aside while preparing bread. (Makes enough for 2 Muffalettas.)

To assemble Muffaletta:

1. Cut bread in half lengthwise. Remove inside soft part of bread and reserve for another use. Leave a 1 inch (2.5 cm) thick shell on both halves.

2. Press 1/4 of the olive salad into bottom of bread. Layer meat and cheese on top of salad. Press another 1/4 of the salad on to meat/cheese layer. Save the second half of the olive salad for your next picnic or make a second muffaletta.

3. Cover with top half of bread. Wrap tightly in plastic wrap.

4. Place a 3-5 pound (1.5-2.5 kg) weight (such as a brick) on top of bread and refrigerate for 8-12 hours.

5. To serve: remove weight, unwrap, slice, and serve.

Serves: 8-10

POLENTA WITH BOLOGNESE SAUCE

This makes a really nice mid-week supper. You can make the thick ragu, or Bolognese sauce, a day or two in advance and simply make the polenta on the night you plan to eat the meal. Add a green tossed salad and some grilled vegetables to round out the meal. Ground veal makes a delicately flavoured Bolognese sauce, but ground beef can also be used.

Bolognese Sauce:

1/4 cup (60 mL) olive oil

3/4 cup (175 mL) finely diced onion

1/2 cup finely (125 mL) diced celery

3/4 cup (175 mL) finely diced carrots

4 garlic cloves, finely minced

2 pounds (1 kg) ground veal (or 1 pound [500g] ground beef and 1 pound [500g] ground veal)

3 cups (750 mL) Chianti or other dry Italian red wine

5 1/2 -ounce (156 mL) can tomato paste

Salt and freshly ground black pepper

1. In a large, heavy-bottomed pot, heat oil over medium high heat. Add onion, celery, and carrots, and sauté, stirring until soft and sauté until soft, about 4-5 minutes. Add garlic and sauté for an additional 1-2 minutes.

2. Add ground veal. Stir constantly, breaking up meat with a wooden spoon, until just cooked, about 5 minutes. Be sure not to 'brown' the veal as this will make the meat tough in the sauce.

3. Add wine and tomato paste and bring to a boil. Reduce heat to low, cover, and simmer until meat is tender and sauce is thickened, about 2 hours. Season to taste with salt and pepper. Stir occasionally.

4. Serve over Polenta.

Continued...

POLENTA WITH BOLOGNESE SAUCE
continued...

Polenta:

1 1/4 cups (310 mL) 2% milk

1 1/4 cups (310 mL) water

1 teaspoon (5 mL) salt

2/3 cup (150 mL) yellow cornmeal

1/2 cup (125 mL) grated Parmesan cheese

1. In a large heavy saucepan, combine milk, water, and salt. Bring to a boil.

2. Starting with a whisk, gradually add cornmeal. You may need to change to a wooden spoon to stir as the mixture thickens. Reduce heat to medium low and stir until polenta is thick and creamy, about 10 minutes. Mix in Parmesan cheese. Season with freshly ground black pepper. Add salt, if necessary.

3. Spoon polenta into a large serving bowl or individual bowls and top with Bolognese sauce.

Serves: 6

CONTINENTAL FONDUE

Most cheese fondues are made with wine, but this is made with beer and the resulting flavour is mellow. Ideal dippers are mini meatballs, bread cubes, and fresh vegetables. I like to steam the vegetables slightly so they are more tender to eat.

8 ounces (250 g) aged Cheddar cheese, shredded

8 ounces (250 g) Swiss Emmenthal cheese, shredded

2 tablespoons (30 mL) all-purpose flour

1/2 teaspoon (2.5 mL) black pepper

1 garlic clove, split open

12 ounces (340 mL) beer of your choice

1 teaspoon (5 mL) Tabasco® sauce

1. Mix cheeses, flour, and pepper in a mixing bowl.
2. Rub inside of fondue pot with garlic.
3. Heat fondue pot and add beer; warm gently.
4. Add cheese mixture one cup (250 mL) at a time; stir to melt after each addition. Add Tabasco® and serve. If mixture becomes too thick, add more beer.

Makes: about 2 cups (500 mL)

HOMEMADE FRESH TORTILLAS

Tortillas are one of the world's many flatbreads. They originated in Mexico and are typically made from wheat or corn. Tortillas cook quickly, often in under two minutes, on a very hot surface such as a griddle or cast iron skillet. Since there is no yeast for leavening, tortillas achieve a temporary leavening when tiny air pockets trapped in the dough are puffed up by rapidly vaporizing steam. Even though they cook rapidly, the surface develops a delicious toasted flavour.

Once you've made these homemade tortillas, you'll never buy them from the store again. They are simple to make, tender, and delicious. You can vary the flavour by adding crushed herbs or spices or make a whole-wheat version by replacing half of the all-purpose flour with whole-wheat flour.

4 cups (1 L) all-purpose flour

2 tablespoons (30 mL) baking powder

2 teaspoons (10 mL) salt

1/4 cup (60 mL) vegetable shortening

1 1/2 cups (375 mL) warm water

1. In a large mixing bowl, stir flour, baking powder, and salt. Cut in shortening until mixture resembles coarse crumbs. Make a well in the centre of the flour mixture. To start, add 1 1/4 cups (310 mL) of the water and stir to form a soft dough. The dough should not be crumbly and should hold together as a ball. Add more water as needed. When a soft dough has formed, remove the dough from the bowl and transfer it to a lightly floured work surface. Knead the dough about 8-10 times.

2. Pinch off a ping pong ball size ball of dough. Roll it very thin with a floured rolling pin. Cover the remaining dough with a damp cloth when not in use.

3. Heat an 8 or 10 inch (20 or 25 cm) cast iron skillet until hot, but not smoking. Do not add fat to the skillet. Reduce heat to medium-high.

4. Place the tortilla on the hot skillet and grill for about 30 to 60 seconds; the tortilla will likely puff-prick with a fork if it does. When the tortilla no longer looks wet and has browned lightly, turn it over, and cook for another 30 to 60 seconds. Transfer to a plate and cover with wax paper.

5. Repeat until all are cooked. Insert wax paper between each tortilla to keep them from sticking.

NOTE: All or part of the dough may be used at once and the remainder stored in the refrigerator for up to 2 days.

Makes: 15-18

NOT SO 'CHILLY' CHILLI!

Don't be put off by the use of canned products here – they're a real time saver in this recipe and add great flavor. You can turn down the heat by using sweet Italian sausage and mild salsa. This recipe can also be finished in a slow cooker. In step 3, place all the ingredients in a slow cooker or crock pot and cook on low for 6-8 hours.

1 pound (500 g) hot Italian sausage, cut into 1 inch (2.5 cm) pieces

2 tablespoons (30 mL) olive oil

2 pounds (1 kg) lean ground beef

1 cup (250 mL) coarsely chopped onion

1 red bell pepper, seeded, deveined and finely chopped

4 garlic cloves, minced

19-ounce (540 mL) can diced tomatoes (including juice)

14-ounce (398 mL) can pork and beans

19-ounce (540 mL) can red kidney beans (including juice)

1 cup (250 mL) homemade or purchased hot salsa

1-2 tablespoons (15-30 mL) chilli powder

1 teaspoon (5 mL) black pepper

1 1/2 cups (375 mL) frozen kernel corn, defrosted and drained

1. In a large skillet, cook sausage in 2 inches (5 cm) of boiling water until cooked; remove from heat and drain; set aside. Clean pan, turn heat to medium high and heat olive oil. And ground beef and brown until no pink remains; remove with a slotted spoon to a medium bowl and set aside.

2. Drain all but 1 tablespoon (15 mL) fat and discard. In the same pan, add onions and peppers to skillet and cook until soft. Add garlic and cook 2 minutes more.

3. In a large ovenproof pot, place cooked sausage, browned ground beef and cooked onion mixture. Add tomatoes, pork and beans, kidney beans, salsa, chilli powder and black pepper. Stir well to combine.

4. Place in preheated 325°F (160°C) oven and cook, covered for 1 1/2 hours. Remove from oven and stir in corn. Cover and return to oven and cook for an additional 1/2 hour.

Serves 8-10

ON-THE-SIDE

Side dishes go a long way to adding balance, colour, crunch, interest, and flavour to a meal. Grains, salads, and vegetables are offered here "On-the-Side."

Cereal grains are often the basis of many side dishes. Ceres is the Roman goddess of agriculture and the root of the word 'cereal'. Common cereal grains include wheat, rice, oats, barley, and corn and some of the lesser known grains include millet, triticale (hybrid of wheat and rye) and wild rice. Many cereal grains are rich sources of dietary fibre as well as a host of vitamins and minerals.

The word 'salad' has its origins in the Latin word for salt, since salt was such an important ingredient in making salad. Today, salads can be made of any variety of fruits, vegetables, meats, or any combination thereof, traditionally topped with some type of moist dressing and tossed together. A composed salad is one that is artfully arranged on an individual plate and then generally drizzled with a dressing.

Vegetables are the edible part of a plant generally cultivated for food purposes. There are a whole host of vegetables ranging in size, shape, color, texture, and nutrition. Some are grown above ground such as broccoli and cauliflower while others take their time growing below ground such as carrots, parsnips, and potatoes. Some foods are called vegetables, such as tomatoes and squash, but botanically, are fruits since they contain one or more seeds. The versatility of vegetables in the culinary world is unparalleled.

ALMOND RICE PILAF WITH LEMON AND THYME

Thyme is a delightful herb native to Southern France and used widely in Mediterranean cuisine. I find it has a real 'earthy' flavour to it. As with many herbs, fresh is best, but thyme is also available in dried leaves and as ground thyme. If fresh is not available, use the dried leaves; try to avoid using ground thyme as I find the flavour can quickly overpower the dish. You can also substitute brown rice in this dish, but you will need more liquid and it will need longer to cook. Generally speaking, when making white rice, the ratio of liquid to rice is 2 cups (500 mL) liquid to 1 cup (250 mL) of rice; for brown rice you need at least 2 1/2 cups (375 mL) of liquid for every 1 cup (250 mL) of rice, and sometimes more depending on the brand of rice. Brown rice adds a nutty texture and more fibre to the dish.

2 tablespoons (30 mL) olive oil

1 1/2 cups (375 mL) raw long grain rice

3 cups (730 mL) simmering chicken stock or broth

2 tablespoons (30 mL) fresh lemon juice

2 sprigs fresh thyme or
1/2 teaspoon (2.5 mL) dried thyme leaves

1 tablespoon (30 mL) finely grated lemon zest

1/2 cup (125 mL) toasted sliced almonds

Chopped fresh parsley, for garnish

1. Heat oil in a large saucepan. Add rice and cook until grains glisten, about 2-3 minutes.

2. Add stock or broth, lemon juice, and thyme sprigs. Bring to a boil. Reduce heat; cover and simmer for 20 minutes or until liquid is absorbed and rice is tender. Remove woody stems from thyme before serving.

3. Stir in lemon zest and toasted almonds. Garnish with chopped parsley.

Serves: 8

CURRIED COCONUT RICE WITH KIDNEY BEANS

In this side dish, hot curry powder, jalapeno pepper, and coconut add complex flavour to otherwise ordinary rice. The kidney beans add fibre, protein, and wonderful colour and texture. It would pair well with curried dishes.

2 tablespoons (30 mL) butter

1 teaspoon (5 mL) hot curry powder

1/2 of a jalapeno pepper, seeded and de-veined, finely chopped

1 medium white onion, coarsely chopped

2 garlic cloves, finely minced

1 1/2 cups (375 mL) raw basmati rice

2 bay leaves

1 teaspoon (5 mL) salt

1/2 cup (125 mL) coconut milk, regular or lite

2 1/2 cups (625 mL) simmering chicken stock or broth

19-ounce (540 mL) can kidney beans, drained and rinsed

1. In a large saucepan on medium heat, melt butter. Add curry powder, pepper, and onion. Sauté until onion is soft. Stir often to ensure curry powder does not scorch. Add garlic and saute 1 minute more. Add rice and cook until grains glisten and become slightly clear. Add bay leaves, salt, coconut milk, and chicken broth.

2. Bring to a boil. Reduce heat to a simmer. Cover and cook 20 minutes or until liquid is absorbed and rice is tender.

3. After 15 minutes of cooking, remove cover and add kidney beans. Stir gently to combine. Return cover to finish cooking. Remove bay leaves prior to service.

Serves: 8

SAFFRON RICE WITH DRIED APRICOTS AND PECANS

Ah, the lore of saffron – that exotic spice that we dare to purchase only when we're ready to splurge! Known as the most expensive spice in North America, it's no wonder that it carries a heavy price tag. It takes over 10,000 hand-picked stigmas from the purple crocus plant to produce one ounce (28 g) of saffron! Thankfully, you only need a tiny amount to produce a distinctive colour and seductive flavour.

Jasmine rice is a fragrant rice that hails from Thailand. Generally speaking, it's less costly than basmati rice and works well as a substitute.

2 tablespoons (30 mL) butter

1 cup (250 mL) raw basmati or jasmine rice

2 cups (500 mL) simmering chicken stock or broth

1 cinnamon stick

1/2 teaspoon (2.5 mL) ground turmeric

6 saffron threads

1 teaspoon (5 mL) salt

Freshly ground black pepper, to taste

1/2 cup (125 mL) coarsely chopped dried apricots

1/2 cup (125 mL) coarsely chopped toasted pecans

1. In a medium saucepan, melt butter. Add rice and stir until grains glisten. Add all remaining ingredients and bring to a boil.

2. Cover and reduce heat to a simmer until all liquid is absorbed and rice is tender, about 20 minutes. Remove cinnamon stick before serving. Leftovers can be served cold the next day as a side salad.

Serves: 6

TURKEY STUFFING WITH SAUSAGE AND HAZELNUTS

Or is it dressing? In my experience, the two terms are used interchangeably. But I tend to think of 'stuffing' as a mixture that is used to 'stuff' a carcass, and a 'dressing' as an accompaniment that is cooked separately. Whatever you choose to call it, this one is delicious and can be cooked in a turkey or baked separately. Every family has their favourite turkey stuffing, and this one is ours.

1 pound (500 g) sweet or hot Italian sausage, casings removed and crumbled into 1/2 inch (1 cm) pieces

1/4 cup (60 mL) butter

2 large yellow onions, coarsely chopped

2 cups (500 mL) coarsely chopped celery

1 tablespoon (15 mL) ground poultry seasoning

1 tablespoon (15 mL) ground sage

1 teaspoon (5 mL) salt

2 teaspoons (10 mL) freshly ground black pepper

12 cups (3 L) day-old whole wheat sandwich bread, crusts removed and cut into 3/4 inch (1.5 cm) cubes (about 1 1/2 loaves store bought bread)

1 cup (250 mL) toasted flaked hazelnuts

1 cup (250 mL) chopped fresh parsley

About 1 cup (250 mL) turkey or chicken stock or broth

1. In a large skillet over medium-high heat, cook sausage completely. Drain fat and discard. Remove sausage to a large bowl.

2. In the same skillet, melt butter and add onions, celery, poultry seasoning, sage, salt, and pepper. Cook until vegetables are tender. Remove from heat and add to the reserved sausage mixture and stir to combine.

3. Place bread, hazelnuts and parsley in a large bowl and stir to combine. Add sausage mixture and toss well. Moisten with 1/2-1 cup (125-250 mL) cold turkey or chicken stock or broth.

4. Makes enough to stuff an 18-pound (8.2 kg) turkey. If you have a smaller bird, don't overstuff it; simply place the extra stuffing into a buttered casserole dish and heat thoroughly.

Serves: 10-12

WILD RICE SALAD WITH DRIED FRUITS AND MINT

Wild rice is not rice at all but rather a long-grain marsh grass native to the Great Lakes region of North America. It's likely called wild rice for its rice-like appearance. It has a wonderful nutty flavour and chewy texture. It goes well in savoury foods such as stuffings and salads. Here, it's accompanied by crunchy nuts, sweet raisins, tart cranberries, and herbs to create a delightful salad. It makes a wonderful addition to a summer buffet table.

1 cup (250 mL) raw wild rice

About 5 cups (1.25 L) chicken broth or water

4 green onions, white part only, finely chopped

1 cup (250 mL) coarsely chopped dried apricots

1 cup (250 mL) coarsely chopped toasted pecans

1 cup (250 mL) golden raisins

1 cup (250 mL) dried cranberries

1/4 cup (60 mL) finely chopped fresh mint (try using different mints such as spearmint for a flavour alternative)

1/4 cup (60 mL) finely chopped fresh basil (do not use dried basil; if you don't have fresh, leave it out)

1/4 cup (60 mL) extra-virgin olive oil

1/3 cup (75 mL) fruit flavoured vinegar such as apple cider or raspberry or use orange juice

1 1/2 teaspoons (7.5 mL) salt

1 teaspoon (5 mL) freshly ground black pepper

1. Cook rice in boiling stock or water until kernels are broken open and tender (about 1 hour). Remove from heat, drain and discard any remaining water and cool.

2. Place cooked cool rice in large mixing bowl. Add all remaining ingredients.

3. Toss gently. Refrigerate for 4-6 hours before service. Serve chilled or at room temperature.

Serves: 8-10

Wild Rice Salad with Dried Fruits and Mint
page 140

Carrot, Raisin, and Chick Pea Salad with Fragrant Spices
page 145

GREEK ORZO SALAD

While the proper name for this pasta is Orzo, I grew up knowing it as Rosa Marina. Why, I'm not sure, but there must be a story here somewhere! Orzo is a rice-shaped pasta that is delicious in soups, but here it takes centre stage in a lovely Mediterranean cold salad. The colour and texture make this a beautiful as well as delicious salad.

1 1/2 cups (375 mL) dry orzo pasta

1/4 cup (60 mL) extra virgin olive oil

1/2 teaspoon (2.5 mL) crushed chilli flakes

1 large red bell pepper, cored, seeded and finely diced

1/2 of a medium English cucumber, skin left on, cut in 1/2 inch (1 cm) dice

1/2 teaspoon (2.5 mL) salt

1/2 teaspoon (2.5 mL) freshly ground black pepper

3/4 cup (175 mL) pitted, coarsely chopped Kalamata olives

3/4 cup (175 mL) crumbled feta cheese

1/2 cup (125 mL) coarsely chopped fresh basil

1/2 cup (125 mL) freshly grated Parmesan cheese

1/2 cup (125 mL) toasted pine nuts

1. In a large pot of boiling salted water, cook orzo pasta until 'al dente'. Drain and place in a large serving bowl. Toss with oil and chilli flakes. Cool to room temperature.

2. Toss in red pepper, cucumber, salt, pepper, and olives. Stir to combine. Add feta, basil, and Parmesan and toss lightly.

3. Top with pine nuts and serve.

Serves: 6-8

BACKYARD POTATO SALAD

The key to the great flavour in this dish is to be sure the vinegar is added to the warm potatoes just after they are cooked. This way, the vinegar penetrates the potato. This recipe takes me back to backyard birthday parties where this salad was always the accompaniment to the traditional hot dogs and hamburgers – it doesn't get much better! Be sure to use a waxy potato such as red new potatoes and not a mealy potato such as Idaho bakers.

2 pounds (1 kg) red new potatoes, eyes removed, skins left on

1/4 cup (60 mL) red or white wine vinegar

1/4 cup (60 mL) finely minced sweet pickles

1/2 cup (125 mL) finely chopped red onion

4 hard boiled eggs, coarsely chopped

8 strips bacon, cooked until crisp and coarsely chopped

1/2 cup (125 mL) finely chopped celery

1/2-1 cup (125-250 mL) regular or fat-reduced mayonnaise

1 teaspoon (5 mL) Dijon mustard

1 teaspoon (5 mL) celery seed

Salt and pepper to taste

2 hard boiled eggs, each cut into 4 wedges, for garnish

1/2 teaspoon (2.5 mL) ground paprika, for garnish

1. Place whole potatoes in a large pot and cover with salted water. Cook until tender and easily pierced with a fork. Drain and let cool about 10 minutes and then dice into 1/2 inch (1 cm) cubes. Place potatoes in large mixing bowl and toss with red wine vinegar. Set aside for about 30 minutes.

2. Add all remaining ingredients to potatoes and toss gently to coat. Season to taste with salt and pepper.

3. To garnish, place boiled egg slices evenly around top of salad and sprinkle with ground paprika.

Serves: 8-10

CARROT, RAISIN, AND CHICK PEA SALAD WITH FRAGRANT SPICES

This is a new twist on an old favourite. The addition of chick peas, onions, and fragrant spices really perks up the traditional carrot and raisin salad. Besides delicious flavour, it has a variety of textures.

8 medium carrots, peeled and cut into 1/4 inch (0.5 cm) coins

2 tablespoons (30 mL) olive oil

1 small onion, thinly sliced

1 teaspoon (5 mL) dried red chilli flakes

1 teaspoon (5 mL) EACH caraway seeds, chilli powder, paprika, ground cumin, and salt

1/2 cup (125 mL) raisins

19 ounce (540 mL) can chick peas, drained

2 teaspoons (10 mL) fresh thyme leaves

1. In a medium sauce pot, cook carrots in boiling water for 3-5 minutes, until tender. Drain and refresh under cold water. Set aside.

2. In a small, non-stick skillet, heat olive oil and cook onions until they begin to limp, about 3-5 minutes. Add spices and cook 1 minute more. Remove from heat and set aside.

3. In a large mixing bowl, combine carrots, cooked onions and spices, raisins, chickpeas and thyme. Stir to combine. Refrigerate until ready to use. Serve chilled or at room temperature. Flavours improve as the salad sits.

Serves: 8-10

CURRIED CHICK PEA SALAD

When adding spices to a dish that is not cooked, such as this salad, be sure the salad stands for several hours prior to service so the full flavour of the spices are released. This salad has wonderful colour, flavour, nutrition, and crunch!

2, 19-ounce (540 mL) cans chick peas, drained

2/3 cup (150 mL) finely diced red onion

2/3 cup (150 mL) finely diced red bell pepper

3 green onions, white part only, finely sliced

2 teaspoons (10 mL) mild or hot curry powder

1/2 cup (125 mL) vegetable oil

3 garlic cloves, finely minced

2 teaspoons (10 mL) finely minced fresh ginger root

3 medium plum tomatoes, coarsely chopped

1/2 cup (125 mL) chopped fresh cilantro

2 tablespoons (30 mL) fresh lime juice

1 teaspoon (5 mL) EACH salt and freshly ground black pepper

3 green onions, green part only, sliced in 1 inch (2.5 cm) diagonals, for garnish

1. In a large mixing bowl, combine all ingredients except garnish. Toss well and refrigerate for 4-6 hours to let flavours develop. Garnish with green onion.

2. Serve chilled or at room temperature.

Serves: 8-10

GERMAN POTATO SALAD

Picking the right potato here is important. There are two types to choose from: mealy and waxy. Mealy potatoes, often called 'bakers' or 'baking potatoes' have a high starch content (they're older and the sugar has turned to starch). They become fluffy when baked and fall apart when boiled, so they are most suited for baking, mashed potatoes, and deep-fried potatoes. Waxy, or new (young) potatoes, have a high sugar and moisture content and are best suited for boiling (they hold their shape and can later be sliced and sautéed or fried). Be sure to use new potatoes in this recipe. This is a family favourite for a backyard barbecue!

3 pounds (about 1.5 kg) medium sized, new red potatoes

1/4 pound (125 g) sliced bacon, chopped in 1/4 inch (.5 cm) dice

1/4 cup (60 mL) white sugar

1/4 cup (60 mL) all-purpose flour

1 tablespoon (15 mL) salt

1/2 teaspoon (2.5 mL) black pepper

1 teaspoon (5 mL) dill seed

1 teaspoon (5 mL) caraway seed

1/2 cup (125 mL) white vinegar

1 cup (250 mL) water

1/2 cup (125 mL) finely diced celery

1/4 cup (60 mL) finely diced green onion, green part only

1/4 cup (60 mL) finely diced green pepper

1. Bring a large pot of salted water to a boil. Add potatoes and cook until fork tender (you can insert and remove a fork with minimal resistance). Cool until they can be handled. Slice into 1/2 inch (1.3 cm) slices and set aside.

2. Preheat oven to 350°F (180°C).

3. In a large skillet, cook bacon until crisp. Remove bacon, crumble, and set aside. Add sugar, flour, salt and pepper to bacon fat in skillet. Stir well to combine; be sure no lumps of flour remain. Add dill, caraway, vinegar, and water, and cook over low heat until thickened. Add celery, onion, and green pepper to sauce in skillet. Stir to combine.

4. Place potatoes and bacon in a lightly greased 12 cup (3 L) casserole dish; add cooked sauce from skillet and stir to combine. Cover and bake for 30-45 minutes or until bubbling and heated through.

Serves: 6-8

BLACK BEAN, ROASTED CORN, AND ROASTED PEPPER SALAD WITH CUMIN DRESSING

There are many popular versions of black bean and corn salad. This one suits my taste as the corn is first roasted to give it a slightly smoky flavour; the roasted peppers add to the subtle flavour. The flavours improve with the marinating time. Any leftover salad can be used as a quesadilla filling or topping for grilled burgers or chicken.

It's also bursting with great nutrition: fibre and protein from the black beans, and vitamin C and antioxidants from the red peppers and tomatoes, all with minimal fat per serving.

For Salad:

2 cups (500 mL) frozen kernel corn, defrosted, drained, and patted dry

2, 19-ounce (540 mL) cans black beans, rinsed and drained

1 cup (250 mL) finely diced red onion

1 cup (250 mL) sliced ripe black olives

1 cup (250 mL) diced roasted red pepper, purchased or home prepared (page 64)

1 1/2 cups (375 mL) diced fresh plum tomatoes

1/2 cup (125 mL) EACH chopped fresh parsley and cilantro

1 cup (250 mL) diced feta cheese

Additional chopped fresh herbs for garnish

Cumin Dressing:

2 tablespoons (30 mL) rice wine vinegar

2 tablespoons (30 mL) balsamic vinegar

1 teaspoon (5 mL) dry mustard

1 1/2 tablespoons (22 mL) ground cumin

1 tablespoon (15 mL) crushed garlic

1/2 cup (125 mL) vegetable oil

1 teaspoon (5 mL) Tabasco® sauce, (more or less to taste)

1 teaspoon (5 mL) salt

1 teaspoon (5 mL) freshly ground black pepper

Continued...

BLACK BEAN, ROASTED CORN, AND ROASTED PEPPER SALAD WITH CUMIN DRESSING

continued...

1. Heat a medium-sized, non-stick skillet over medium-high heat. Do not add oil. Add kernel corn and toast it until it starts to blacken. Be careful, as some kernels may 'pop'. Remove from heat and set a side to cool.

2. In a large mixing bowl, combine cooled corn with black beans, red onion, black olives, roasted red pepper, tomatoes, parsley, and cilantro, and gently mix.

3. In another small mixing bowl or dressing shaker, combine vinegars with dry mustard and mix well. Add remaining dressing ingredients and mix or shake well.

4. Pour dressing over salad ingredients and stir to combine. Let marinate in the refrigerator for 4-12 hours. Transfer to serving bowl. Just before service, top with feta cheese and garnish with additional fresh herbs.

Serves: 10-12

GRAPE TOMATO SALAD WITH OLIVES, CUCUMBERS, AND FENNEL

You can almost feel the warm Mediterranean breeze when you enjoy this simple salad in your backyard! Grape tomatoes are a wonderful recent addition to North American markets. A cross between a roma, tear-drop, and cherry tomato, grape tomatoes are grown in clusters, like grapes, and have a wonderful sweet flavour and firm texture. Because of their size (1/2-3/4 inch [1-1.5 cm]) and low juice content, their 'squirt factor' is low and they are easily a one-bite food. Use good quality extra-virgin olive oil in this salad to enhance its flavour.

Salad:

3 cups (750 mL) grape tomatoes

1 cup (250 mL) Kalamata or sun-dried black olives, pitted and quartered, if desired

1/2 of an English cucumber, sliced in quarters lengthwise, and then cut into 1/2 inch (1 cm) slices

1/2 of a small fennel bulb, trimmed and cut into very thin strips

1 cup (250 mL) finely diced red onion

1/4 cup (60 mL) chopped fresh basil

Italian Vinaigrette:

1/4 cup (60 mL) balsamic vinegar

1/2 teaspoon (2.5 mL) dried mustard

1/4 teaspoon (1.25 mL) salt

1/2 teaspoon (2.5 mL) EACH dried basil and oregano

2 garlic cloves, finely minced

1/3 cup (75 mL) extra virgin olive oil

Freshly ground black pepper

To assemble:

1. Combine all salad ingredients in a mixing bowl.

2. To make vinaigrette, in a separate bowl, whisk together balsamic vinegar, mustard, salt, garlic, and herbs. Slowly add olive oil to combine. Season this vinaigrette with pepper to taste.

3. Drizzle vinaigrette over salad and serve. Flavour improves if marinated for 4-6 hours.

Serves: 6-8

PINK GRAPEFRUIT AND AVOCADO SALAD WITH POPPY SEED DRESSING

Sectioning a grapefruit is one of those tasks that we think of as difficult, but it's really quite simple with a bit of practice. Start by placing the grapefruit stem side up on a cutting board. With a very sharp knife, begin to remove the skin from top to bottom; get close to the flesh so that all the skin is removed. Continue to work around the grapefruit until all the skin is removed and you have a lovely naked fruit. Now, start to 'section' the grapefruit: slip a sharp knife right next to the membrane and begin to remove each section. Place sections into a small bowl as they are removed. You can also use white grapefruit, but the pink flesh makes a very pretty salad.

In this recipe, make sure the spinach is dried very well, so the dressing can properly adhere to the leaves.

Salad:

8 cups (2 L) washed and dried baby spinach

1 small red onion, sliced into very thin rings

2 pink grapefruits, peeled; grapefruit sections cut out and white membranes discarded

1 large ripe avocado, peeled, seeded, and sliced into 1/2 inch (1 cm) slices

1 small red, orange, or yellow bell pepper, seeded, cored, and sliced into very thin strips

Poppy Seed Dressing:

1/2 cup (125 mL) seasoned rice vinegar

1/2 cup (125 mL) fresh pink grapefruit juice

1/2 cup (125 mL) extra virgin olive oil

1/4 cup (60 mL) poppy seeds

1 tablespoon (15 mL) sugar

Salt and freshly ground black pepper, to taste

To assemble:

1. Divide spinach leaves evenly on 8 plates. Arrange red onion, grapefruit, avocado, and bell pepper attractively on top of spinach.

2. For dressing, whisk vinegar and grapefruit juice together. Whisk in olive oil. Add poppy seeds, sugar, and salt and pepper to taste. Pour dressing evenly over salads.

Makes: 8 first course salads

SPINACH SALAD WITH FRESH NECTARINES, RASPBERRIES, AND CANDIED ALMONDS

Here's a delightful way to use the fresh fruits of summer. You can also use fresh peaches, strawberries, or blueberries. Be sure the fruits are fully ripe.

Salad:

6 cups (1.5 L) baby spinach

2 large fully ripe nectarines, pitted, sliced into 6 wedges and then diced

1 cup (250 mL) fresh raspberries

3 green onions, white part only, thinly sliced

Dressing:

1/3 cup (75 mL) mayonnaise, regular or fat-reduced

1/2 cup (125 mL) peach yogurt

1 tablespoon (15 mL) honey

2 tablespoons (30 mL) raspberry vinegar

1 tablespoon (15 mL) poppy seeds

1/2 cup (125 mL) candied almonds, for garnish

To assemble:

1. Divide spinach among 6 salad plates. Attractively arrange nectarines, raspberries, and green onions.

2. For dressing, in a small bowl, combine all ingredients and mix well. Pour dressing over salads. Garnish with candied almonds. Serve chilled.

To make candied almonds, place 1/2 cup (125 mL) sliced almonds in a hot, medium non-stick skillet. Sprinkle with 1/3 cup (75 mL) white sugar and stir to coat. Continue to cook over medium heat until sugar starts to melt. Stir constantly to coat almonds with caramelizing sugar. When almonds are fully coated with caramelized sugar, remove from heat and place on waxed paper or parchment paper, being sure to break up the nuts so they don't stick together.

Serves: 6

GLAZED BEETS WITH BALSAMIC VINEGAR AND ROSEMARY

The colour in beets can stain many surfaces including towels (often a permanent stain) and sometimes even countertops and skin (generally a temporary stain), so take care when preparing. I often wear plastic gloves to protect my skin and cover the countertop with newspaper while preparing beets.

Root vegetables lend themselves well to roasting. In this recipe, the sugar and balsamic vinegar provide ingredients for caramelizing the beets, which gives them a sweet yet slightly tart flavour.

2 pounds (1 kg) beets, peeled and cut into 1 inch (2.5 cm) cubes

2 teaspoons (10 mL) vegetable oil

1/4 cup (60 mL) balsamic vinegar

2 tablespoons (30 mL) brown sugar

1/2 cup (125 mL) water

1 sprig fresh rosemary

1/4 cup (60 mL) snipped chives

1. Preheat oven to 375°F (190°C). Spray a small roasting pan with cooking spray. Place beets in pan, cover, and bake about 1 hour until fork tender. Turn occasionally.
2. Heat oil in a large non-stick skillet over medium-high heat. Add beets and stir to coat with oil.
3. Stir in balsamic vinegar, brown sugar, water, and rosemary. Cook over medium heat until water evaporates and sugar begins to caramelize, about 10 minutes. Stir frequently.
4. Season with salt and pepper and garnish with fresh chives. Remove rosemary stem before serving.

Serves: 6

MARION'S JAVA BAKED BEANS

This tried and true old recipe comes from the mother of a friend of mine at work. The addition of coffee gives it a truly unique, almost smoky taste.

4 slices bacon, cut into 1/2 inch (1 cm) pieces

1 medium onion, thinly sliced

1/3 cup (75 mL) brown sugar

1 teaspoon (5 mL) instant coffee granules dissolved in 1 tablespoon (15 mL) water

1 teaspoon (5 mL) white or apple cider vinegar

1 teaspoon (5 mL) dry mustard

1/2 teaspoon (2.5 mL) salt

1 teaspoon (5 mL) ground black pepper

2, 14-ounce (398 mL) cans pork and beans

1. Preheat oven to 350°F (180°C).

2. In a small skillet over medium heat, cook bacon until fat is released and bacon is still chewy, but not crisp. Add onions and cook until onions are soft, about 5 minutes. Add brown sugar, dissolved coffee granules, vinegar, dry mustard, salt and pepper. Stir until sugar dissolves, about 3 minutes. Remove from heat.

3. Place pork and beans in a medium casserole dish. Add bacon/onion mixture and stir to combine. Cover and bake for 1 hour, taking the cover off and stirring the beans 15 minutes prior to the end of cooking.

Serves: 8-10

PAN-STEAMED SPINACH WITH GARLIC AND SESAME SEEDS

Since spinach has a lot of water in it, when you add heat to it, it wilts quickly and cooks down to less than a quarter of what you started with! You will need about 1-1 1/4 pounds (500-625 g) of spinach to get the 10 cups (2.5 L) for this recipe. Note too that in this recipe, you need to leave a little water on the spinach – this is what creates the steam to wilt it during cooking, so even if you buy pre-washed spinach, run it quickly under cold water so as to get a little water on it. Conversely, if you were washing spinach for use in a salad, you want to dry it completely, so that the dressing sticks to the leaves.

1 tablespoon (15 mL) vegetable oil

1 teaspoon (5 mL) sesame oil

4 garlic cloves, finely minced

10 cups (2.5 L) baby spinach, rinsed under cold water; do not dry (the remaining water droplets will help to steam the spinach)

1/4 cup (60 mL) sesame seeds lightly toasted in 350°F (180°C) oven or in a saucepan on the stove top (be careful not to burn)

Salt and freshly ground black pepper, to garnish

1. In large skillet, heat olive and sesame oil over medium heat and sauté garlic for 1 minute until fragrant; do not burn. Add spinach and cover skillet. Steam spinach for 1-2 minutes until wilted. Check and stir often so it doesn't burn or turn to olive green.

2. Remove to serving bowl season with salt and pepper. Garnish with toasted sesame seeds.

Serves: 6

ROASTED VEGGIES WITH SOY AND GARLIC

I've made this dish several times for our good friends at dinner parties and we always end up fighting over who gets the garlic! Garlic roasted in its skin becomes very sweet and mellow. You can add as much garlic as you like in this dish. I've been known to use two entire bulbs for certain guests!

1 pound (500 g) white or yellow baby potatoes, cut into 1 inch (2.5 cm) pieces

1 pound (500 g) carrots, peeled and cut into 1 inch (2.5 cm) pieces

2 medium white onions, each cut into 6 wedges

1 pound (500 g) small beets, peeled and cut into wedges

1 pound (500 g) parsnips, peeled and cut into 1 inch (2.5 cm) pieces

1/3 cup (75 mL) vegetable oil

1/3 cup (75 mL) soy sauce

12 garlic cloves, NOT peeled

1. Preheat oven to 400°F (200°C).
2. In a 9x13 inch (3 L) baking pan, toss vegetables to combine. Sprinkle with oil and soy sauce and stir. Scatter garlic cloves over vegetables. Cover with aluminum foil and cook for 30 minutes. Uncover, turn vegetables, and continue to cook another 15-20 minutes or until vegetables are fork tender.
3. Remove from pan and serve.

Serves: 6-8

SAUTÉED MUSHROOMS WITH SHALLOTS AND FRESH THYME

Shallots are a member of the onion family, but they look more like large garlic. They range in colour from light brown to pale rose. To prepare, their papery outer leaves and root should be removed and they should be cut like an onion. They are available year round, but unfortunately, tend to be costly. In this dish, however, they are really worth the splurge.

Since mushrooms release water when they cook, it's easy to 'stew' the mushrooms instead of sautéing them. To ensure they sauté and brown nicely, be sure the mushrooms are dry when you begin cooking and that the pan is hot and not overcrowded.

1/4 cup (60 mL) butter

1/2 pound (250 g) EACH white and brown mushrooms, sliced 1/4 inch (0.5 cm) thick

1 teaspoon (5 mL) olive oil

1 teaspoon (5 mL) Worcestershire sauce

1/4 cup (60 mL) finely minced shallots

2 garlic cloves, finely minced

4 sprigs fresh thyme, stripped and finely chopped to yield about 2 teaspoons (10 mL) thyme leaves

Salt and freshly ground black pepper

2 tablespoons finely snipped chives, for garnish

1. Heat a large non-stick skillet on medium-high heat and add 2 tablespoons (30 mL) of the butter. Add half of the mushrooms. Cook, without stirring, until mushrooms start to brown. Give the pan a 'flip' to turn the mushrooms over and continue to sauté for 1-2 more minutes. Transfer mushrooms to a serving dish and set aside to keep warm.

2. Repeat with remaining butter and mushrooms; remove from pan and add to first batch and keep warm.

3. In the same pan over medium heat, heat olive oil and Worcestershire sauce. Add garlic, shallots, and thyme. Sauté 1-2 minutes, being careful not to burn the garlic. Add reserved sautéed mushrooms to the pan; stir well and heat through for 3-4 minutes. Season to taste with salt and freshly ground pepper. Garnish with fresh chives.

This is a perfect accompaniment to Herb-Crusted Tenderloin of Beef, (page 80)

Serves: 8

SWEET CURRIED CARROTS

Sweet dates are nicely complemented with curry in this interesting and unusual fruit and vegetable combination. Slivered almonds are the result of taking the whole almond and cutting them from top to bottom in wedges to create 'slivers'. In contrast, sliced or flaked almond are cut much thinner. Slivered almonds hold up better in this dish.

2 tablespoons (30 mL) butter

1/3 cup (75 mL) pitted, chopped dates

2 pounds (1 kg) carrots, cut in 1/2 x 2 inch (1 x 5 cm) matchsticks

1 teaspoon (5 mL) brown sugar

2 teaspoons (10 mL) curry powder

Salt and black pepper, to taste

1/3 cup (75 mL) slivered almonds, lightly toasted

1. In a large skillet, melt butter and sauté dates slightly. Add carrots, brown sugar, and curry powder. Cook until carrots are tender, about 8-10 minutes.

2. Season with salt and freshly ground black pepper. Remove from skillet and garnish with toasted slivered almonds.

Serves: 6

Maple Walnut Pie
page 186

Baked Winter Fruits with Spiced Wine
page 181

SWEET ENDINGS

In English class, I could always remember that dessert had ' 2 s's' because I often wanted two servings!

The range of desserts available in the culinary world today is almost breathtaking. Dessert can be as simple and delicious as sliced fresh summer fruits or as elaborate as towers of chocolate. For me, dessert must be homemade. Nothing irritates me more than being out to dinner at a lovely restaurant, only to be served a dessert that's obviously been made a long time ago by a machine many miles away.

Desserts including cookies, cakes, pies, and pastries can have a place in a healthy meal plan provided the ground rule of moderation applies. The desserts provided here include a range of cookies, squares, cakes, pies, and fancy desserts that are sure to please any palate and keep you lingering at the table to enjoy conversation.

COWBOY COOKIES

I have no idea why these are called 'cowboy' cookies – that's the way Mom gave me the recipe!

Coconut trees grow in the hot climates of Malaysia, South America, India, and Hawaii to a ripe old age of 70 years and produce thousands of coconuts along the way. Botanically a fruit, the coconut is one of few non-animal products rich in saturated fats. You can tell this because when you leave coconut oil at room temperature, it turns solid. You may have seen solids at the top of a can of coconut milk, which is the hard saturated fat. Despite its fat content, coconut adds wonderful flavour to these cookies. Conversely, the walnuts in this recipe are a source of healthy unsaturated fat and also provide some fibre.

1 cup (250 mL) soft butter
1/2 cup (125 mL) white sugar
1/2 cup (125 mL) dark brown sugar
2 large eggs
1 1/2 teaspoons (7.5 mL) vanilla extract
2 cups (500 mL) all-purpose flour
1 1/2 teaspoons (7.5 mL) baking soda
1 teaspoon (5 mL) baking powder
1/2 teaspoon (2.5 mL) salt
2 cups (500 mL) quick cooking oats
1 cup (250 mL) sweetened long flake coconut
1 cup (250 mL) finely chopped walnuts or pecans
1 1/2 cups (375 mL) semi-sweet chocolate chips

1. Preheat oven to 350°F (180°C). Lightly grease 2 large cookie sheets and set aside.
2. In a large mixing bowl, beat butter and sugars until light and fluffy. Add eggs and vanilla. Beat well. Add flour, baking soda, baking powder, and salt. Blend well.
3. Stir in oats, coconut, nuts, and chocolate chips. Mix until well blended.
4. Drop cookies by 2 tablespoons (30 mL) onto lightly greased cookie sheets. Bake for 12-15 minutes or until cookies spring back when touched with a finger.

Makes: 3 dozen

MOLASSES SPICED COOKIES

You'll think you have way too much flour as you make these cookies, but carry on – they work like a charm and make a very tender and flavourful old-fashioned cookie. I've tried making it with butter, but the result is not satisfactory. Depending on where you live, the amount of flour you need will vary; you'll need the lesser amount of flour if you live in a dry climate and the larger amount if you live in a moist climate. The resulting dough should be smooth and stiff, but not dry.

1 cup (250 mL) vegetable shortening

1 cup (250 mL) white sugar

1 large egg

1 cup (250 mL) fancy molasses

1 cup (250 mL) boiling water with 2 teaspoons (10 mL) baking soda

5 1/2-6 cups (1.1-1.25 L) all-purpose flour

2 teaspoons (10 mL) EACH ground cinnamon, ginger, and nutmeg

1/4 cup (60 mL) white sugar for sprinkling on cookies

1. Preheat oven to 375°F (190°C). Lightly grease 2 large cookie sheets and set aside.
2. In a large mixing bowl, beat shortening and sugar until light and fluffy, about 3-4 minutes. Add egg and molasses. Beat 1 more minute.
3. In another mixing bowl, combine flour and spices.
4. Alternately add boiling water mixture and flour mixture to form a smooth and stiff dough.
5. Drop dough by 2 tablespoons (30 mL) onto prepared cookie sheets. Sprinkle each cookie with a little white sugar. Bake for 10-12 minutes or until tops spring back when touched with a finger. Remove from oven and transfer to cooling rack.

Makes: about 36 cookies, depending on how large you make them

PEPPERMINT WHOOPIE PIES

A whoopie pie is native to the Pennsylvania Dutch culture and thought to have been created by using up leftover cake batter. It's traditionally made of two small, chocolate, disk-shaped cakes with a sweet, creamy frosting sandwiched between them. I've offered my favourite version with a peppermint filling which nicely complements the rich chocolate cake. The use of dark cocoa powder makes these cakes very dark and delicious. If you can't find it in your area, regular cocoa powder works just as well. These should be eaten soon after they're filled – that's not usually a problem!

2 cups (500 mL) all-purpose flour

3/4 cup (175 mL) dark cocoa powder

1/2 teaspoon (2.5 mL) baking powder

1 teaspoon (5 mL) baking soda

3/4 teaspoon (3.75 mL) salt

1 cup (250 mL) buttermilk (3.25% or 1%MF)

2 teaspoons (10 mL) vanilla extract

1/2 cup (125 mL) soft butter

1 cup (250 mL) lightly packed, light brown sugar

1 large egg

1. Preheat oven to 350°F (180°C). Line two large baking sheets with parchment paper and set aside.
2. Into a medium mixing bowl, sift the flour and cocoa powder. Add baking powder, baking soda and salt. Stir to combine and set aside.
3. In a small bowl, combine buttermilk and vanilla.
4. In a large mixing bowl, cream butter, brown sugar, and egg until light and fluffy. Add flour mixture alternately with buttermilk mixture until well blended.
5. Drop mixture by 1/4 cup (60 mL) measures onto the prepared baking sheets, leaving approximately 2 inches (5 cm) between each cookie.
6. Bake for about 15 minutes or until the cookies spring back when lightly touched. Transfer to cooling racks. Cool completely before filling.

Continued...

DEVIL'S FOOD PEPPERMINT WHOOPIE PIES
continued...

Peppermint Filling:

1/2 cup (125 mL) soft butter

1/2 cup (125 mL) icing sugar

2 cups (500 mL) marshmallow cream

1 teaspoon (5 mL) peppermint extract

Few drops red food colouring (optional)

1. In a medium mixing bowl, cream butter with sugar until light and fluffy. Stir in marshmallow cream, extract, and food colouring (if using) and combine well.

Assembly:

Spread half of the cakes with 2 tablespoons (30 mL) filling on the flat side. Press flat side of another cake to make the whoopie pie.

Makes: 18-24 whoopie pies

HALF MOONS

This is the recipe I've created for those delightful cookies that my dad used to bring home for me from our favourite bakery. They're very close to perfect in both taste and looks. Enjoy them for a treat on a special occasion.

3/4 cup (175 mL) soft butter

1 1/2 cups (375 mL) sugar

2 large eggs

3 1/2 cups (975 mL) all-purpose flour

1 teaspoon (5 mL) baking soda

1 teaspoon (5 mL) baking powder

1/2 teaspoon (2.5 mL) salt

1/2 teaspoon (2.5 mL) ground nutmeg

1 teaspoon (5 mL) vanilla extract

1 cup (250 mL) buttermilk (3.25% or 1% MF)

1. Preheat oven to 350°F (180°C). Lightly grease two large cookie sheets or line with parchment paper.
2. In a large mixing bowl, cream butter and sugar until light and fluffy. Add eggs and blend well.
3. In a medium bowl, combine flour, baking soda, baking powder, salt, and nutmeg.
4. In a small bowl, stir together vanilla and buttermilk.
5. Add flour mixture alternately with buttermilk mixture to creamed butter mixture until well combined.
6. Scoop 1/3 cup (75 mL) portions of batter and drop onto prepared baking sheets. Try to keep the dough evenly shaped and be sure to keep about 2 inches (5 cm) apart as they will spread.
7. Bake for 20-25 minutes or until tops spring back when lightly touched. Let cool 5 minutes and then transfer to cooling rack, turning upside down so the smooth bottom has now become the top. Frost with vanilla and chocolate icing.

Continued...

HALF MOONS
continued...

For icing:

1/4 cup (60 mL) soft butter

4 cups (1 L) icing sugar

1/2 cup (125 mL) 2% milk

1 teaspoon (5 mL) vanilla extract

2, 1-ounce (30 g) squares unsweetened chocolate, melted and cooled

1. In a large mixing bowl, cream butter and sugar. Add milk and vanilla and cream until very smooth and spreadable. You may need to add either milk to make it thinner or icing sugar to make it thicker.

2. Divide icing in half and place in two separate bowls. To one bowl, add the cooled chocolate and stir to combine.

3. Frost 1/2 of each moon-shaped cookie with white icing, forming a semi-circle. Frost the other 1/2 of the cookie with the chocolate icing.

Makes: 16-18 large cookies

DREAM CAKE SQUARES

These delightful squares start with a shortbread base and then are topped with delicious fruits and nuts and finally frosted with a citrus icing – a perfect addition to a holiday dessert table. Cut the squares very small (1 inch [2.5 cm]) squares as they are very rich.

Base:

1 cup (250 mL) all-purpose flour
2 tablespoons (30 mL) icing sugar
1/2 cup (125 mL) soft butter

Filling:

1 cup (250 mL) candied (glacé) cherries
1 cup (250 mL) walnuts or pecans
1/2 cup (125 mL) sweetened long flake coconut
1/4 cup (60 mL) all-purpose flour
1/2 teaspoon (2.5 mL) baking powder
Dash of salt
2 large eggs, lightly beaten
1 cup (250 mL) light brown sugar, lightly packed
1/2 teaspoon (2.5 mL) vanilla extract

Icing:

1 tablespoon (15 mL) soft butter
1 cup (250 mL) icing sugar
1 tablespoon (15 mL) orange juice
1 tablespoon (15 mL) lemon juice
1/2 teaspoon (2.5 mL) vanilla extract

Continued...

DREAM CAKE SQUARES
continued...

For base:

1. Preheat oven to 350°F (180°C).

2. Combine flour, butter, and icing sugar in a small mixing bowl. Blend thoroughly and press into the bottom of a lightly greased 8x8 inch (2 L) square baking pan. Bake about 10 minutes until lightly puffed. Remove from oven and cover with filling.

For filling:

1. In a food processor, pulse cherries and nuts until coarsely ground (cherries are about 1/4 inch [0.5 cm]). Remove to a medium mixing bowl and add coconut, flour, baking powder, and salt.

2. In another small bowl, combine eggs, brown sugar, and vanilla. Pour egg mixture over fruit mixture and stir well to combine. Pour evenly over partially cooked base. Return to oven and cook for an additional 25-30 minutes. Remove from oven and cool.

3. When completely cool, cover with icing.

For icing:

1. In a small bowl, combine butter and icing sugar. Add orange juice, lemon juice, and vanilla. Stir to make a smooth icing. Spread icing evenly over cooled bars. When icing is set, cut into 1 inch (2.5 cm) squares.

Makes: about 4 dozen squares

LEMON SLICE

It seems everyone has their take on lemon slice, and this one has been tried and true for me. I like my lemon slice thick, so I use an 8 inch (2 L) square baking pan for this recipe. It can be made in 9 inch (2.5 L) square pan, but the baking time will need to be slightly reduced. It can be quite a challenge to cut as the lemon filling gets sticky. To make the job easier, be sure to dip your knife in hot water or spray it with a cooking spray each time you cut a slice.

Base:

1 1/2 cups (375 mL) all-purpose flour

3/4 cup (175 mL) icing sugar

Pinch salt

3/4 cup (175 mL) butter

Filling:

1 1/2 cups (375 mL) white sugar

3 large eggs

1/2 cup (125 mL) fresh lemon juice

For base:

1. Preheat oven to 350°F (175°C). Lightly grease an 8 inch (2 L) square baking pan.

2. In a medium mixing bowl, combine flour, icing sugar, and salt. Stir to combine. Cut in butter with a pastry cutter or two butter knives until mixture resembles coarse crumbs. Transfer mixture to baking pan. Pat down lightly to even out base. Bake for 20 minutes. Remove from oven and cover with filling.

For filling:

1. While base is baking, in a medium mixing bowl, combine sugar and eggs. Beat well until creamy, about 5-7 minutes. Slowly add lemon juice and continue to beat.

2. After base has finished baking, pour lemon filling mixture over base. Return to oven and continue to bake about 25 minutes or until sides and top are browned and centre of mixture is set.

3. Remove from oven and cool on cooling rack. Cut into squares and serve.

Makes: about 16 squares

PEANUT BUTTER OATMEAL COOKIES WITH CHOCOLATE CHIPS

The kids will just love these gems. You can make them into a giant or 'monster' cookie if you like, but increase the baking time by a few minutes to allow for the larger cookie.

1/2 cup (125 mL) soft butter

1 cup (250 mL) lightly packed light brown sugar

1 cup (250 mL) white sugar

3 large eggs

1 teaspoon (5 mL) vanilla extract

1 1/2 cups (375 mL) chunky peanut butter

4 1/2 cups (1.125 L) quick cooking oats mixed with 2 teaspoons (10 mL) baking soda

1 cup (250 mL) chocolate chips

1 cup (250 mL) Smarties® candies

1. Preheat oven to 325°F (160°C). Lightly grease 2 large baking sheets or line with parchment paper.

2. In a large mixing bowl, beat butter with sugars until light and fluffy. Beat in eggs, vanilla, and peanut butter until well blended. Stir in oat mixture until a stiff dough forms. Stir in chocolate chips and candies.

3. Form into 2 inch (5 cm) balls for large cookies (or 1 inch [2.5 cm] balls for medium) and place on prepared baking sheet. Flatten slightly.

4. Bake for 15-17 minutes for large cookies (about 12 minutes for medium). Remove from oven and let cool 1-2 minutes before removing and transferring to cooling rack.

Makes: 24 medium or 12-15 large cookies

SPICY BONBONS

These have graced many wedding dessert tables in my hometown. The spice comes from cloves, allspice, cinnamon, and, believe it or not, black pepper! You'll think you've done something wrong when you get a very stiff dough – but that's the way the dough should be. These cookies also do not spread out, but rather retain their round 'ball' shape. My best friend always asks for 'bonbons, please' when she visits.

4 cups (1 L) all-purpose flour

1 cup (250 mL) white sugar

1/2 cup (125 mL) unsweetened cocoa powder

1 teaspoon (5 mL) EACH ground cloves, allspice, cinnamon, and black pepper

2 teaspoons (10 mL) baking powder

1/2 teaspoon (2.5 mL) baking soda

1/2 teaspoon (2.5 mL) salt

1 teaspoon (5 mL) vanilla extract

1/2 cup (125 mL) vegetable oil

1 cup (250 mL) 2% milk

1 cup (250 mL) finely chopped nuts, such as walnuts or pecans

3-4 ounces (90-120 mL) whisky, such as rye or scotch

1. Preheat oven to 350°F (180°C). Lightly grease 2 large baking sheets.

2. In a large mixing bowl, combine flour, sugar, cocoa powder, spices, baking powder, baking soda, and salt. Stir well. Add vanilla, oil, and milk. Mix on medium speed (or by hand) until well blended and very stiff. Add nuts and blend well.

3. Add whisky until batter becomes pliable and dough-like. At this stage, you should be able to form the mixture into firm balls that hold their shape.

4. Pinch off dough and roll into 1 inch (2.5 cm) balls. Place on lightly greased cookie sheets. Bake for 12 minutes. Cookies will feel firm to the touch, but not solid throughout.

5. Remove from oven; let cool 5 minutes and then transfer to cooling rack. Cool completely before frosting.

Continued...

SPICY BONBONS
continued...

Frosting:

4 cups (1 L) confectioners sugar

1/2 cup (125 mL) unsweetened cocoa powder

5 tablespoons (75 mL) vegetable oil

2 tablespoons (60 mL) vanilla extract

2 ounces (60 mL) whisky
(same type used in the cookies)

About 1/2 cup (125 mL) cold, strong coffee

1. In a large mixing bowl, combine sugar, cocoa, oil, vanilla, and whisky. Slowly add coffee until a thick, spreadable frosting consistency is achieved.

2. Frost cookies generously and set aside on cooling rack to let frosting 'set'.

Makes: 5-6 dozen cookies

BISCOTTI WITH ALMONDS, DRIED APRICOTS, AND WHITE CHOCOLATE

Biscotti are baked twice, which gives them extra crunch. They're ideally suited for dipping in coffee or sweet wine after dinner.

1/3 cup (75 mL) soft butter

3/4 cup (175 mL) white sugar

2 large eggs

2 1/4 cups (560 mL) all-purpose flour

1 1/2 teaspoons (7.5 mL) baking powder

1 teaspoon (5 mL) salt

1 1/2 teaspoons (7.5 mL) anise seed

1 tablespoon (15 mL) finely grated orange zest

1 teaspoon (5 mL) vanilla extract

1/2 teaspoon (5 mL) almond extract

1 cup (250 mL) finely chopped dried apricots

1/2 cup (125 mL) chopped flaked almonds

3/4 cup (175 mL) chopped white chocolate pieces (not chips)

1. Preheat oven to 325°F (160°C). Line a large baking sheet with parchment paper.
2. In a large mixing bowl, beat butter with sugar until light and fluffy. Add eggs and beat well.
3. In a small bowl, stir to combine flour, baking powder, salt, and anise seed.
4. Add flour mixture, zest, and extracts to egg/sugar mixture and mix well.
5. Stir in apricots, almonds, and white chocolate pieces, and stir to incorporate into dough.

Continued...

BISCOTTI WITH ALMONDS, DRIED APRICOTS, AND WHITE CHOCOLATE

continued...

6. Transfer dough to clean work surface. Divide in half. Shape each half into 2 inch (5 cm) wide by 9 inch (23 cm) long by 1 inch (2.5 cm) high logs. Place on prepared baking sheet (well spaced from each other). Bake for 30-35 minutes.

7. Remove from oven and cool on baking sheet for 10 minutes. Remove from baking sheet to clean cutting board.

8. Cut into 1 inch (2.5 cm) wide biscotti. Return biscotti to baking sheet, cut side down, and bake an additional 10 minutes. Remove from oven. Remove from baking sheet to cooling racks and cool completely.

Makes: 18-24 biscotti

POPULAR DEMAND PEANUT COCONUT BALLS

My children tried these cookies at a friend's house over the Christmas holidays and they quickly became a family favourite. They're simple to make and are a must-have if you're a fan of coconut.

1 cup (250 mL) smooth peanut butter

1 cup (250 mL) graham wafer crumbs

1 cup (250 mL) icing sugar

1. In a large mixing bowl, stir together the peanut butter, wafer crumbs, and icing sugar. When the dough starts to come together, transfer it to a clean work surface and work it well by kneading it until the mixture is smooth and pliable (if it is too dry, then add a bit more peanut butter).

2. Roll into small 3/4 inch (1.5 cm) balls and set aside on a clean baking sheet. Prepare icing.

Icing:

1 tablespoon (15 mL) soft butter

1 cup (250 mL) icing sugar

1 teaspoon (5 mL) vanilla extract

Enough milk to make a very thin icing that will adhere to peanut butter balls

2 cups (500 mL) sweetened long flake coconut

1. In a small mixing bowl, cream butter. Add icing sugar and vanilla. Mix until smooth. Add enough milk to make a very thin icing.

Assembly:

To frost, place one ball on a fork and dip in icing; roll around to coat. Alternatively, you can spoon the icing over the balls. Roll in sweetened coconut and let dry on waxed paper.

Makes: 5-6 dozen balls

Peppermint Whoopie Pies

page 164

Dessert Squares

Popular Demand Peanut Coconut Balls page 176
Spicy Bonbons page 172
Dream Cake Squares page 168

COCOA BEAN BITES

And you thought this recipe used cocoa beans! Nope – it uses red kidney beans as the base. Don't dismay; you'll never taste or see a kidney bean, but you will have all the delicious nutrition from them.

2 cups (500 mL) quick cooking oats

1 cup (250 mL) barley flour (use all-purpose if you can't find barley flour)

1 teaspoon (5 mL) baking powder

1/2 teaspoon (2.5 mL) baking soda

1/2 cup (125 mL) unsweetened cocoa powder

1 teaspoon (5 mL) ground cinnamon

1/2 teaspoon (2.5 mL) ground cloves

1/2 teaspoon (2.5 mL) salt

19-ounce (540 mL) can red kidney beans, rinsed and drained

2 tablespoons (30 mL) water

1/3 cup (75 mL) soft butter

1 cup (250 mL) lightly packed light brown sugar

2 large eggs

1 teaspoon (5 mL) vanilla extract

3/4 cup (175 mL) chocolate chips

1. Preheat oven to 350°F (180°C). Lightly grease two large baking sheets.
2. In a large mixing bowl, combine oats, barley flour, baking powder, baking soda, cocoa powder, cinnamon, cloves, and salt. Stir to combine.
3. Place beans in a food processor with water and pulse until smooth. Transfer to a large mixing bowl. Add butter and cream on medium speed with mixer until well blended. Add brown sugar, eggs, and vanilla. Beat until smooth, scraping down the side of the bowl occasionally.
4. Add dry ingredients and mix until blended. Stir in chocolate chips.
5. Drop by 2 tablespoonfuls (30 mL) onto prepared baking sheets. Bake for 14-16 minutes until slightly firm to the touch. Transfer to cooling racks.

Makes: 30-36 cookies

BERRY PEACHY CRISP

You can just taste summer in this fruity crisp. Of course you can substitute other fruits, but I find this combination to be my favourite. If you prefer your peaches peeled for this dish, simply bring a large pot of water to boil and then reduce to a simmer. Submerge the fresh peaches in simmering water and cook for 1-2 minutes. Test if the skin is ready to be removed by taking a peach out of the water and peeling back the skin. If it pulls away easily, it's done. When this occurs, transfer to a large bowl of cold water to stop the cooking process. As soon as you're able to handle the fruits without burning your hands, remove the skin from the peaches with a sharp paring knife.

Topping:

3/4 cup (175 mL) lightly packed brown sugar

3/4 cup (175 mL) all-purpose flour

1/3 cup (75 mL) cold butter

1 cup (250 mL) large flake oats

3/4 cup (175 mL) chopped walnuts or pecans

Fruit Mixture:

1/3 cup (75 mL) sugar

3 tablespoons (45 mL) all-purpose flour

1/2 teaspoon (2.5 mL) ground cinnamon

1/4 teaspoon (1.25 mL) ground nutmeg

3 1/2 pounds (about 1.6 kg) fresh peaches, pitted and diced into 1 inch (2.5 cm) cubes (optional to peel them if you like)

2 cups (500 mL) fresh blueberries

For topping:

1. In a medium mixing bowl, combine sugar and flour and mix till blended. Using a pastry cutter or two butter knives cut in butter until coarse crumbs form. Stir in oats and pecans until well blended. Set aside.

For fruit mixture:

1. Preheat oven to 350°F (180°C). Lightly grease a 9x13 inch (3 L) baking dish.

2. In a large mixing bowl, combine all ingredients. Mix well. Transfer fruit to prepared baking pan and cover with crisp topping.

3. Bake in preheated oven for 45 minutes until bubbling. Remove from oven. Serve warm with fresh peach, cinnamon, or vanilla ice cream.

Serves: 8-12

BAKED WINTER FRUITS WITH SPICED WINE

This is a fabulous way to get delicious fruit in the middle of winter. Drying is a way to preserve fruit where nearly 80% of the moisture is removed. In drying fruit, the sweetness and flavour becomes very concentrated, so you often don't need much to get full flavour. Dried fruits should be stored tightly wrapped in a plastic bag at room temperature. They can be eaten as is, or as in this recipe, reconstituted with liquid.

1 1/2 cups (375 mL) dry white wine

1 cup (250 mL) lightly packed brown sugar

1 tablespoon (15 mL) finely diced candied ginger

1 teaspoon (5 mL) vanilla extract

1/2 teaspoon (2.5 mL) EACH ground cinnamon, allspice, and ginger

1 lemon, grated zest and juice of

1 pound (500 g) dried apricot halves, cut into quarters

1 pound (500 g) assorted other dried fruit such as peaches (cut into quarters), cranberries, raisins, or prunes (cut into quarters)

2 tablespoons (30 mL) butter

1 cup (250 mL) chopped walnuts or pecans

1. Lightly butter an 8 cup (2 L) glass or ceramic baking dish and set aside. In a medium mixing bowl, combine wine, brown sugar, ginger, vanilla, spices, lemon juice, and zest. Blend well and set aside.

2. In a large bowl, combine all dried fruits. Transfer half of fruit to prepared baking dish. Dot with 1 tablespoon (15 mL) butter and sprinkle with half the nuts. Spread remaining fruit and dot with remaining butter and nuts. Pour wine mixture over all fruit and nuts. Cover with plastic wrap and refrigerate at least 8 hours or overnight. Remove fruit from refrigerator and warm slightly on the counter for 1 hour, remove plastic wrap.

3. Preheat oven to 350°F (180°C). Cover with aluminum foil. Bake for 20 minutes. Remove foil, stir fruit, and continue to bake until fruit is plump and liquid is caramelized, about 20 minutes more.

4. Remove from oven and serve warm over vanilla ice cream or frozen yogurt.

Serves: 8-10

SPICED CARROT CAKE

This recipe took several tries to get it perfect, and indeed I think it is! The fat is substantially reduced compared to the usual carrot cakes, and all the flavour is preserved. The icing is also lower in fat than most varieties as there's no added butter. Give it a try for your next ladies luncheon.

2/3 cup (150 mL) white sugar

2/3 cup (150 mL) vegetable oil

2 large eggs

1/2 cup (125 mL) unsweetened applesauce

2 1/4 cups (625 mL) all-purpose flour

1/2 teaspoon (2.5 mL) salt

1 teaspoon (5 mL) ground cinnamon

1/4 teaspoon (1.25 mL) ground cloves

1 teaspoon (5 mL) baking soda

1 teaspoon (5 mL) baking powder

2 cups (500 mL) lightly packed grated carrots

1/2 cup (125 mL) coarsely chopped pecans or raisins

1. Preheat oven to350°F (175°C). Lightly grease and flour a 9x13 inch (3 L) baking pan.

2. In a large mixing bowl, combine sugar and oil. Blend well. Add eggs and applesauce. Blend.

3. In a separate bowl, stir together flour, salt, spices, baking soda, and baking powder. Add to sugar mixture. Beat well to combine. Add carrots, pecans or raisins and blend well. Pour into prepared baking pan and bake for 25-30 minutes or until cake tester inserted into centre of cake comes out dry. Cool for at least 2 hours and then dust with icing sugar or frost with cream cheese icing.

Cream Cheese Icing:

2/3 cup (150 g) fat-reduced cream cheese, at room temperature

1 1/2 cups (375 mL) icing sugar

1. In a medium mixing bowl, beat cream cheese until smooth. Beat in icing sugar and mix until smooth. Spread on cooled cake.

Serves: 12

PERFECT PASTRY CREAM FOR CREAMED PIES

Here's a never-fail way to make pastry cream. I always struggled with scorching pastry cream when I made it, but a talented (and handsome!) pastry chef taught me this technique, which thickens the cream quickly.

4 cups (1 L) 2% milk

2/3 cup (150 mL) white sugar

1/2 cup (125 mL) butter

3 large eggs

2 large egg yolks

2/3 cup (150 mL) cornstarch

2/3 cup (150 mL) white sugar

1 teaspoon (5 mL) vanilla extract

1. In a medium saucepan, combine milk, sugar, and butter. Bring to a boil.
2. In a large mixing bowl, combine eggs, egg yolks, cornstarch, and sugar. Mix until smooth.
3. Add egg mixture to boiling milk mixture all at once, stirring constantly. Mixture will begin to thicken quickly. Stir constantly and boil for about 30-60 seconds. Remove from heat. Stir in vanilla.

Makes: about 5 cups (1.25 L) pastry cream; enough for two, 8 inch (20 cm) pies or one, 9 inch (23 cm) deep dish cream pie

To make CHOCOLATE CREAM PIE, add 4, 1-ounce (30 g) squares melted unsweetened chocolate to hot pastry cream and stir to combine. Place in cooled baked 9 inch (23 cm) pie shell; refrigerate until ready to use.

To make COCONUT CREAM PIE, add 1 1/2 cups (375 mL) long flake coconut to pastry cream and stir to combine. Place in cooled baked 9 inch (23 cm) deep dish pie shell. Refrigerate until ready to use. If desired, toast an additional 1/2 cup (125 mL) coconut to garnish.

To make BANANA CREAM PIE, layer fresh bananas and pastry cream in cooled baked 9 inch (23 cm) deep dish pie shell, starting and finishing with pastry cream. Refrigerate until ready to use.

STRAWBERRY SHORTCAKES

These shortcakes have been in my family for years. When they're made, we know summer has arrived.

Don't over mix the biscuit dough or it will be tough.

2 cups (500 mL) all-purpose flour

1/4 cup (60 mL) white sugar

1 tablespoon (15 mL) baking powder

1/2 teaspoon (2.5 mL) salt

1/2 cup (125 mL) COLD butter

1 large egg

2/3 cup (150 mL) whole or 2% milk

2 tablespoons (30 mL) white sugar for sprinkling

1. Preheat oven to 425°F (215°C). Lightly grease one large baking sheet.

2. In a large mixing bowl, stir together flour, sugar, baking powder, and salt. Cut in butter with a pastry blender or two butter knives until mixture is the size of small peas.

3. In a small bowl, whisk egg and add milk. Add to flour mixture and stir until mixture holds together.

4. Drop by large spoonfuls onto prepared baking sheet to make 8-10 large shortcakes. Sprinkle tops with 1/2 teaspoon (2.5 mL) each white sugar. Bake for 10-12 minutes or until slightly browned.

5. To serve, cut tops off shortcakes, fill with berries, replace top, and add whipped cream if desired.

Continued...

STRAWBERRY SHORTCAKES
continued...

Strawberries:

4 cups (1 L) fresh ripe strawberries, hulled

1/2 cup (125 mL) white sugar (more or less to taste, depending on sweetness of berries)

In a large bowl, slice berries. Add sugar and stir. Let sit for about 1 hour for berries to get juicy.

Cream:

1 cup (250 mL) whipping cream

1/4 cup (60 mL) icing sugar

1/2 teaspoon (2.5 mL) vanilla extract

In a large, cold mixing bowl, whip cream with beaters until frothy; add sugar and Vanilla, and continue to beat until stiff peaks form. Do not over beat!

Serves: 8-10

MAPLE WALNUT PIE

Here's a delightful pie filled with the goodness of oats and the sweet flavour of maple syrup and coconut.

1/2 cup (125 mL) white sugar
1/2 cup (125 mL) brown sugar
1/2 cup (125 mL) melted butter
3/4 cup (175 mL) quick-cooking oats
1/2 cup (125 mL) pure maple syrup
2 large eggs
1 teaspoon (5 mL) vanilla extract
1 cup (250 mL) sweetened long flake coconut
1/2 cup (125 mL) buttermilk (3.25% or 1% MF)
1/2 cup (125 mL) raisins
1 cup (250 mL) coarsely chopped walnuts
9 inch (23 cm) unbaked pie shell

1. Preheat oven to 425°F (215°C).
2. In a large mixing bowl, combine sugars, melted butter, oats, maple syrup, eggs, vanilla, coconut, and buttermilk. Stir until well combined. Stir in raisins and nuts. Pour into unbaked pie shell and bake for 10 minutes. Reduce heat to 375°F (190°) and bake an additional 30 minutes or until top is firm to the touch.
3. Cool completely before cutting. Serve with vanilla or maple walnut ice-cream.

Serves: 6-8

TORTONI

This recipe goes back as far as I can remember in my mother's home. It's a very simple traditional Italian dessert that can be made up to two weeks prior to service and kept in the freezer. You can vary the flavours of the added fruits and nuts to your liking.

2 egg whites, room temperature

2/3 cup (150 mL) icing sugar, divided in half

1 cup (250 mL) whipping cream

2 tablespoons (30 mL) brandy or rum

2 tablespoons (30 mL) finely chopped toasted pecans, pine nuts, or pistachios

2 tablespoons (30 mL) sweetened long flake coconut

2 tablespoons (30 mL) finely chopped maraschino cherries

2 tablespoons (30 mL) mini chocolate chips

1. Line 12 muffin cups with paper liners.
2. In a medium stainless steel or glass mixing bowl, beat egg whites until foamy. Gradually add half of the icing sugar and beat until stiff peaks form. Set aside.
3. In another medium mixing bowl, whip cream until soft peaks form. Add remaining half of the icing sugar and beat until stiff peaks form. Fold in brandy or rum and beaten egg whites. Fold in nuts, coconut, cherries, and chocolate chips.
4. Fill prepared baking cups to the top with mixture. Cover with plastic wrap and freeze until firm. Remove from freezer 15 minutes prior to service.
5. Serve with biscotti if desired.

Makes: 12

CHRISTINE'S SELF-SAUCING LEMON PUDDING

Christine is the mom of a friend of mine and a fabulous cook. This is one of those really old-fashioned desserts that's wonderful any time of the year. Try to use fresh lemon juice if you can as it really enhances the flavour. A few fresh raspberries or blueberries on the side complement the lemon flavour and add to the presentation.

As the dish cooks, the bottom half magically develops into a lovely, flavourful cake, while the top half stays a velvety, lush pudding. It is quite simply amazing!

2 tablespoons (30 mL) soft butter plus
1 teaspoon (5 mL) for greasing bowl

7/8 cup (220 mL) white sugar

3 large eggs, separated

1 cup (250 mL) whole or 2% milk

1 1/2 tablespoons (22 mL) all-purpose flour

1/3 cup (75 mL) fresh lemon juice

Finely shredded zest of 1 lemon

1. Preheat oven to 350°F (180°C). Lightly butter a 6 cup (1.5 L) deep casserole dish with 1 teaspoon (5 mL) butter and set aside.

2. In a medium mixing bowl, cream 2 tablespoons (30 mL) butter and sugar. Gradually add egg yolks and continue to cream for 1 more minute. Add milk, flour, lemon juice, and zest. Beat to mix well. Set aside.

3. In another small stainless steel or glass mixing bowl, beat egg whites until soft peaks form. Fold whites into lemon mixture. Place mixture into prepared casserole dish.

4. Place in a water bath (set casserole dish filled with pudding into a larger casserole dish; fill larger dish halfway with water). Bake for 45 minutes until firm to the touch.

5. To serve, scoop pudding into individual serving dishes so that the soft 'pudding' is on the top and drizzles over the cake layer formed on the bottom of the dish.

Serves: 6

DATE AND NUT LOAF

The date palm tree is the oldest known food on the planet, dating back to 50,000 BC. Still today, we can enjoy the sweet fruit of this tree. I always remember this as one of the treats my mother would serve to the girls on bridge night. Cut this loaf into slices and serve with cream cheese for a true taste sensation.

1 cup (250 mL) chopped pitted dates
1 cup (250 mL) boiling water
1 teaspoon (5 mL) baking soda
1/2 cup (125 mL) vegetable shortening
1 cup (250 mL) white sugar
1 large egg
1 teaspoon (5 mL) vanilla extract
1 2/3 cup (325 mL) all-purpose flour
1 cup (250 mL) finely chopped walnuts or pecans

1. Place dates in a small bowl. Cover with boiling water. Add shortening and baking soda. Set aside for 1 hour.
2. Preheat oven to 300°F (150°C). Lightly grease and flour 2, 9x5 inch (2 L) loaf pans and set aside.
3. In a large mixing bowl, beat sugar and egg. Add vanilla and flour and blend well. Add date mixture and blend well. Stir in nuts until well mixed.
4. Turn batter into prepared loaf pans and evenly distribute.
5. Bake for about 1 hour or until tester inserted into centre of loaves comes out dry.
6. Remove from oven and let cool for 1 hour on cooling racks before removing from pan.
7. To serve, cut into 1 inch (2.5 cm) slices. Spread lightly with cream cheese if desired.

Makes: 2 loaves

INDEX

A

B